The Pitchforks Are Coming

What Happens When the 99% Say 'Enough'?

Sean Hogan

Dedication

To those who have fought for justice, equity, and fairness in the face of adversity.

To the workers, the reformers, the visionaries, and the truth-tellers who refuse to accept a world where wealth and power are hoarded by the few at the expense of the many.

To my family, friends, and colleagues who have supported me throughout my journey, offering wisdom, encouragement, and unwavering belief in the pursuit of a better world.

And to future generations—may they inherit a world that values dignity over greed, progress over division, and humanity over profit.

Acknowledgments

Writing *The Pitchforks Are Coming* has been a journey shaped by the insights, support, and encouragement of many individuals.

First and foremost, I extend my deepest gratitude to my family, whose unwavering belief in me and constant encouragement have been a source of strength throughout this process. Your patience and support have made this book possible.

To my friends and colleagues who have engaged in countless discussions, debates, and reflections on the themes of this book—your perspectives have challenged and refined my thinking. Your contributions, whether direct or indirect, have left an indelible mark on these pages.

I would also like to acknowledge the scholars, economists, and historians whose work has provided the intellectual foundation for much of this book. Their research and analyses have been invaluable in shaping the arguments and insights presented here.

A special thanks to those who have dedicated their lives to advocating for economic justice and systemic reform. Your work is a testament to the power of resilience and the pursuit of a fairer world.

I am particularly grateful to Nick Hanauer, whose thought-provoking TED Talk, *Beware, Fellow Plutocrats, the Pitchforks Are Coming*, first inspired me to explore these ideas in greater depth. His insights on economic inequality and the risks of wealth concentration have played a significant role in shaping my thinking and this book.

Finally, to the readers—whether you agree, disagree, or find yourself somewhere in between—I appreciate your willingness to engage with these ideas. It is through open dialogue, critical thought, and collective action that meaningful change becomes possible.

Thank you all.

About the Author

Sean Hogan is a seasoned leader in corporate governance, public service, and economic policy. With a distinguished career spanning multiple sectors—including infrastructure, finance, and regulatory affairs—he has served as a board director, chairman, and strategic advisor for numerous organizations. His expertise in corporate accountability, economic equity, and systemic reform has shaped his perspective on the growing wealth divide and its consequences for modern society.

Over the years, he has worked at the intersection of business and public service, navigating complex challenges in governance, strategic planning, and stakeholder engagement. His tenure in leadership roles has given him firsthand insight into the structures that concentrate wealth and power—insights that form the foundation of *The Pitchforks Are Coming*.

Beyond his corporate experience, he has long been a student of history, political economy, and social justice movements. His work is driven by a deep commitment to addressing wealth inequality, fostering sustainable economic policies, and advocating for structural reforms that prioritize human dignity over unchecked financial gain.

This book is the culmination of his decades of experience, research, and reflection on the forces shaping our world today. It serves as both a warning and a roadmap—an urgent call to action for those who believe that a fairer, more just society is not just possible but necessary.

When not writing or working on governance and policy matters, Sean Hogan is an advocate for sustainability and infrastructure reform, particularly in the areas of water, energy, and public services. He remains actively engaged in thought leadership on corporate ethics, economic justice, and the future of capitalism.

The Pitchforks Are Coming is his contribution to the ongoing conversation about inequality, power, and the future of democracy.

Preface

The concentration of wealth is not a new phenomenon, but in the 21st century, it has reached levels that threaten the stability of economies and societies worldwide. As technological advancements accelerate and financial markets become more complex, the divide between the wealthy elite and the rest of society continues to widen.

In this book, I have tried to explore the root causes, historical precedents, and potential consequences of wealth inequity while examining how economic systems have evolved to create such disparities—and what can be done to address them.

As we enter 2025, disillusionment in the United States has reached a boiling point. Economic inequality has deepened, wages have stagnated, and the cost of living has soared, further eroding the financial security of ordinary citizens. At the same time, corporate elites wield unprecedented power, fuelling widespread distrust in institutions and intensifying political polarisation.

Across the country, from small towns to major cities, people are questioning whether the American Dream still exists. Many are turning to populist movements—on both the left and right—searching for answers in a system that seems rigged against them. Protests, social unrest, and calls for systemic change are growing louder, signalling that we are at a critical juncture.

History teaches us that when societies ignore the grievances of the many in favour of the privileges of the few, they do so at their own peril. This book seeks to examine these fault lines, exploring how we arrived at this moment and what must be done to forge a more equitable future.

The warning signs are not unique to the United States. Across Europe and beyond, we see the resurgence of far-right movements, increased voter apathy, and declining trust in democracy. Economic frustration has been a driving force behind Brexit, mass protests in France, and growing authoritarianism in parts of Eastern Europe.

The political instability that results from rising inequality does not simply threaten economic progress—it undermines the very foundations of democracy. If economic policies continue to disproportionately favour the elite, the political backlash will only grow stronger, and history shows us that these moments often lead to radical, and sometimes violent, upheaval.

My journey in writing this book began in 2014 when I first encountered Nick Hanauer's TED Talk, which sparked my curiosity and concern about the growing gap between the rich and the rest of society. His warning—that unchecked wealth accumulation would eventually lead to public revolt—resonated deeply.

Over the years, I have observed these issues firsthand throughout my career as a worker, manager, board director, and chairman. Having spent seventy years on this earth, my experiences have provided me with a unique perspective on the realities of wealth distribution and the challenges that arise from unchecked economic disparities. This book is the culmination of my reflections, observations, and ongoing research into one of the most pressing issues of our time.

The economic shifts of the past few decades have been deeply personal as well. Like many, I have watched working people struggle under the weight of stagnant wages, unaffordable housing, and a shrinking social safety net. Many of these struggles are not due to a lack of effort or skill but rather the result of a system designed to extract maximum profit at the expense of everyday people.

As I progressed in my own career and gained firsthand experience with corporate governance and financial decision-making, I saw the ways in which wealth is concentrated and protected, often to the detriment of workers and small businesses. These experiences shaped my understanding of the forces that drive inequality and the urgent need for reform.

I wanted this book to be concise and accessible. I wasn't aiming for *War and Peace* but rather a straightforward, readable exploration of my life observations, my understanding of the world we live in, and practical ideas for how we can collectively build a better future. My goal is simply to provide insights that are easily understood and applied by readers from all walks of life.

History teaches us that extreme wealth concentration has consequences. The collapse of monarchies, the fall of empires, and the rise of revolutionary movements have all been driven by economic injustice. When the gap between the rich and the rest grows too large, societies become unstable, and power structures that once seemed unshakable can collapse overnight.

The French Revolution, the Russian Revolution, and, more recently, the Arab Spring all serve as reminders that economic discontent can quickly turn into political upheaval. Yet, despite these historical warnings, we continue to see the same patterns playing out today.

The modern economy has become increasingly skewed in favour of the wealthy and powerful, with policies that erode labour protections, suppress wages, and undermine workers' rights. Governments continue to roll back safeguards, allowing corporations to prioritise profits over people and leaving millions in precarious conditions.

Wages stagnate while executive bonuses soar, and the social contract that once provided stability is slowly being dismantled. This book is a warning, but it is also a call to action—because if history has taught us anything, it is that no system built on inequality can endure indefinitely.

At the same time, I believe that change is possible. The economic system is not a force of nature—it is built by people and can be changed by people. Throughout history, societies have successfully challenged entrenched power structures and rewritten the rules of wealth and opportunity.

Progressive taxation, labour rights, and social welfare programmes were all once radical ideas that became widely accepted solutions. Today, we are at another inflection point where bold reforms are needed to ensure economic stability and social cohesion.

This book is not merely a diagnosis of the problem but a roadmap for change. By understanding the mechanisms that drive wealth accumulation, the impact of deregulation and tax policies, and the role of social movements in shaping economic policy, we can begin to chart a course towards a more just and sustainable future.

The choices we make today will determine whether we repeat the mistakes of the past or seize the opportunity to create a fairer economic landscape for future generations.

As you read through these pages, consider the broader implications of wealth concentration—not just for economies, but for democracy, social cohesion, and the very fabric of our communities. The pitchforks may not be coming today, but they are dangerously close.

If we fail to address the warning signs, history tells us what comes next. But there is still time. By working towards a more equitable and sustainable economic system, we can prevent the upheaval that follows when too much wealth and power are concentrated in too few hands.

Change is inevitable—the question is whether we choose to guide it or wait until it is forced upon us.

Part I

Introduction:
A Message from Within.

Nick Hanauer's Message to Fellow Zillionaires

Nick Hanauer, a Seattle-based entrepreneur and venture capitalist, made waves in 2014 with his provocative essay, *The Pitchforks Are Coming... For Us Plutocrats*. His message was simple yet powerful: unchecked inequality is not just a moral failure—it is a practical and existential threat to the wealthy elite who benefit from it. Hanauer's words resonated because they came from someone who had directly profited from the systems he criticised. As a billionaire, his critique of wealth concentration carried weight, signalling a rare instance of self-reflection among the plutocratic class.

Hanauer's arguments rest on two core ideas: the unsustainable nature of wealth inequality and the inherent fragility of a society where the vast majority feel excluded from prosperity. His essay, which was as much a plea as it was a warning, emphasised that if inequality continues unabated, social and economic upheaval will inevitably follow. This section of my book delves into Hanauer's message, his supporting arguments, and its broader implications for society.

The Unsustainability of Wealth Inequality

Hanauer's critique begins with a fundamental observation about economic systems: they rely on consumers to drive growth. He argues that the super-rich, by hoarding wealth, undermine this dynamic. Unlike the middle and working classes, who spend a significant portion of their income, the wealthy save or invest most of their earnings. While this may generate returns for individuals, it does little to stimulate broader economic activity.

He often uses a simple but effective metaphor to explain this: the economy is like an ecosystem. In a healthy forest, sunlight and nutrients reach all levels, from the tallest trees to the smallest plants. If a few trees grow too tall and block out the sun, the undergrowth withers, and the entire system begins to collapse. This ecological analogy underscores the importance of balance. When wealth is concentrated in too few hands, it disrupts the economic "photosynthesis" that keeps society thriving.

One of his most pointed criticisms is directed at the "trickle-down economics" narrative. He calls it a "dangerous delusion" that has convinced generations of policymakers to prioritise tax cuts for the wealthy and deregulation for corporations. This approach, he argues, ignores the reality that demand—not supply—is the true engine of economic growth. Without consumers who can afford to spend, businesses fail, and the economy stagnates.

Historical Parallels and Warnings

Hanauer bolsters his argument by drawing parallels to historical moments of upheaval caused by inequality. One of his most striking comparisons is to the French Revolution, a period when economic disparity reached a breaking point. The ruling elite of pre-revolutionary France ignored the suffering of the masses until it was too late. What followed was not just a redistribution of wealth but a complete dismantling of the existing order, with many aristocrats paying the ultimate price.

This historical precedent serves as a chilling warning for modern plutocrats. Hanauer cautions that revolutions are not always neatly ideological or predictable. The masses, when pushed to desperation, may not distinguish between the "good" and the "bad" among the elite. Instead, they may seek wholesale retribution, leading to chaos and destruction that benefits no one.

Hanauer also points to the early 20th century in the United States as a cautionary tale. During the Gilded Age, industrialists like Rockefeller and Carnegie amassed unprecedented wealth, while the working class toiled in dire conditions. The economic inequality of this era fuelled widespread labour unrest, including strikes and violent clashes. The reforms of the Progressive Era, such as the establishment of labour rights and antitrust laws, were not born out of altruism but necessity—an attempt to stave off revolutionary fervour.

The Role of the Elite in Preventing Collapse

Hanauer's essay is not merely a critique; it is a call to action. He urges his fellow billionaires to recognise their self-interest in addressing inequality. His argument is pragmatic: redistributing wealth and investing in social programmes are not acts of charity but investments in long-term stability.

One of Hanauer's key proposals is raising the minimum wage. He argues that putting more money into the hands of workers would create a "virtuous cycle" of growth, as increased consumer spending drives demand for goods and services. While many business leaders claim that higher wages would harm profitability, Hanauer counters that a well-paid workforce is essential for sustainable capitalism.

In addition to wage reforms, Hanauer advocates for progressive taxation, stronger labour protections, and investments in education and infrastructure. These measures, he believes, would help rebuild the middle class, which has historically been the backbone of prosperous societies. He also calls for a shift in corporate culture, urging businesses to prioritise stakeholders—workers, communities, and the environment—over shareholders.

Resistance and Criticism

Hanauer's message has not been universally embraced, particularly among his peers in the billionaire class. Critics accuse him of oversimplifying complex economic issues and underestimating the role of innovation and entrepreneurship in creating wealth. Some argue that his proposed solutions, such as higher taxes and wage mandates, could stifle economic growth or drive businesses to relocate.

Despite this pushback, Hanauer's arguments have gained traction among policymakers and activists. His essay helped popularise the idea that inequality is not just a moral issue but a practical one with tangible consequences. Movements like *Fight for $15* in the US, which advocates for a higher minimum wage, echo many of his ideas.

The Broader Implications

Hanauer's warning is not just for the wealthy elite—it is for society as a whole. His essay challenges us to rethink the assumptions that underpin our economic systems. If left unchecked, inequality threatens not only economic stability but also democracy itself. When citizens feel excluded from prosperity, they lose faith in institutions and turn to populist leaders who promise quick fixes, often at the expense of long-term stability.

Hanauer's message is a reminder that we are all interconnected. The health of an economy depends on the well-being of its participants. By addressing inequality, we can create a more resilient, inclusive society that benefits everyone—not just the privileged few.

The Ticking Time Bomb of Inequity

Inequity, particularly in terms of wealth distribution, has always been a fundamental fault line in societies throughout history. Today, however, the scale and complexity of inequity have reached unprecedented levels, creating conditions ripe for social and political upheaval.

The current global economic system has produced staggering levels of wealth for a small fraction of the population, while the vast majority continue to struggle with stagnating wages, rising living costs, and diminishing social mobility. This growing divide represents a ticking time bomb—one that, if left unchecked, could lead to widespread unrest, institutional collapse, and a reshaping of societal structures in ways we are only beginning to comprehend.

The Unprecedented Wealth Gap

In recent decades, the concentration of wealth has become more extreme than at any point in modern history. The wealthiest 1% of the global population now controls nearly half of the world's total wealth, while the bottom 50% owns just a fraction. This disparity is not merely a statistical anomaly; it is a reflection of systemic failures in our economic and political institutions. The mechanisms of capitalism, once heralded for driving innovation and opportunity, have instead become tools for wealth consolidation, benefiting those who are already at the top while leaving the majority behind.

The rapid acceleration of technological advancements has exacerbated these divides. Automation and artificial intelligence have displaced millions of jobs, disproportionately affecting low- and middle-income workers. Meanwhile, the digital economy rewards those with access to capital and education, further entrenching existing inequalities. The result is a society where upward mobility is increasingly out of reach for many, leading to frustration and disillusionment.

Erosion of Social Cohesion

Wealth inequity does not exist in isolation; it has profound effects on social cohesion and trust in institutions. As the gap widens, so too does the sense of alienation among those left behind. The middle class, traditionally considered the backbone of economic stability and democratic governance, is shrinking. This decline has eroded confidence in traditional political systems, leading to the rise of populist movements that thrive on dissatisfaction and resentment. This is something I will cover further in my next book, *The Politics of Rage*.

Historically, societies with extreme wealth disparities have struggled to maintain social harmony. When a small elite controls most of the resources, public trust in fairness and justice deteriorates. This manifests in declining voter participation, widespread cynicism towards political leadership, and, in more extreme cases, civil unrest. Protests against economic inequality, such as the Occupy Wall Street movement or the Gilets Jaunes in France, illustrate the growing frustration with a system perceived as rigged in favour of the wealthy elite.

The Economic Consequences of Inequity

Beyond its social and political ramifications, wealth inequity poses significant risks to economic stability. Economists have long argued that sustained economic growth relies on a healthy and thriving middle class. When wealth is concentrated at the top, consumer spending—the lifeblood of modern economies—declines. Those with immense wealth are less likely to spend proportionally compared to those with lower incomes, leading to weaker demand, slower economic growth, and ultimately, economic stagnation.

Furthermore, wealth inequity stifles innovation and entrepreneurship. In a fair system, opportunities for economic advancement should be based on merit and effort. However, when capital and resources are concentrated in the hands of a few, access to essential resources such as education, healthcare, and capital investment becomes increasingly restricted for the majority. This limits social mobility and hinders the potential for new ideas and businesses to emerge, further entrenching the cycle of inequality.

Political Responses and Failures

Governments worldwide have struggled to address the growing inequity crisis effectively. Policy interventions, such as progressive taxation, social welfare programmes, and minimum wage adjustments, have had limited success in reversing the tide. In many cases, political inertia and corporate influence have diluted efforts to create meaningful change. Meanwhile, austerity measures introduced in response to economic crises have disproportionately harmed the most vulnerable, deepening the divide between the rich and poor.

Moreover, globalisation has presented unique challenges for policymakers. The ability of corporations and wealthy individuals to move capital across borders has undermined national efforts to tax wealth fairly. Countries find themselves in a race to the bottom, offering tax incentives and deregulation to attract investment—often at the expense of their own citizens' well-being.

The Warning Signs

There are clear warning signs that inequity is reaching a breaking point. Increasing social polarisation, declining mental health, and rising crime rates in economically depressed areas are just a few indicators that society is under strain. Social media has amplified the voices of the disaffected, providing a platform for grievances and, in some cases, enabling the radicalisation of those who feel left behind by the current system.

History teaches us that when inequality reaches unsustainable levels, revolution—or at least radical societal change—becomes inevitable. The French and Russian revolutions, both driven by extreme economic disparities, serve as cautionary tales. In the modern era, the Arab Spring demonstrated how economic discontent could quickly spiral into widespread political upheaval.

The Arab Spring, which began in late 2010 and swept across the Middle East and North Africa, was a stark reminder of how economic inequality, political corruption, and public frustration can ignite mass uprisings. While rooted in regional grievances, the movement was heavily influenced by the ideals of democracy and social justice championed by the United States. However, the effects of the Arab Spring did not remain confined to the Middle East; the images of people rising up against oppressive regimes resonated deeply within the U.S., fuelling domestic movements like Occupy Wall Street.

In turn, the Arab Spring was also influenced by the growing economic frustrations in the West, as protesters across the Middle East cited corporate greed, financial inequality, and systemic corruption as sources of their own discontent. This cyclical exchange of discontent illustrates how economic and political unrest knows no borders—inequity and repression, wherever they exist, ultimately provoke resistance and revolution.

Addressing the Time Bomb

The path forward requires a concerted effort from governments, businesses, and civil society. Addressing inequity must go beyond token gestures and focus on systemic change. Policies aimed at wealth redistribution—such as universal basic income, wealth taxes, and comprehensive public services—must be seriously considered. Education and skills training must be prioritised to ensure that the workforce is equipped to adapt to the evolving economy.

Ultimately, the challenge is to build a fairer system that balances economic growth with social equity. Failure to do so will not only perpetuate existing inequalities but may also trigger the very societal breakdown that history warns us about. The ticking time bomb of inequity is not an abstract threat—it is a reality that demands urgent and decisive action.

Understanding Wealth Concentration in the 21st Century

Wealth concentration is one of the defining features of the 21st-century global economy. Despite significant technological and economic advancements, the accumulation of wealth in the hands of a few has reached unprecedented levels, deepening socio-economic divides and posing serious challenges to the sustainability of economies and democracies alike.

The mechanisms driving this concentration are multifaceted, influenced by economic policies, technological disruptions, and the ever-growing influence of multinational corporations and financial institutions. Understanding the forces behind wealth concentration is essential to addressing its impacts and developing solutions that promote equitable economic growth.

The Historical Context of Wealth Accumulation

While wealth accumulation is not a new phenomenon, its acceleration in the 21st century is unparalleled. Historically, wealth was concentrated in the hands of monarchies, aristocracies, and colonial empires. However, the post-industrial era brought new opportunities for wealth creation and distribution. In the mid-20th century, economic policies aimed at redistributing wealth through taxation, social welfare programmes, and labour rights led to a more balanced distribution of wealth in many developed nations.

Since the late 20th century, however, a shift towards deregulation, globalisation, and financialisation has reversed many of these gains. The rise of neoliberal economic policies, which prioritise free markets and minimal government intervention, has facilitated the accumulation of wealth by corporations and individuals at the top of the economic hierarchy.

Deregulation, Tax Havens, and Policy Failures

Deregulation has played a significant role in exacerbating wealth concentration by removing critical safeguards that once ensured fair economic competition and worker protections. Over the past few decades, governments worldwide have relaxed regulations designed to prevent monopolistic behaviour, enforce fair wages, and ensure corporate accountability. This deregulation has allowed corporations to prioritise profit maximisation with fewer constraints, often at the expense of workers, small businesses, and the environment.

The financial sector has been one of the primary beneficiaries of deregulation. Policies aimed at reducing regulatory oversight have allowed banks and investment firms to engage in speculative activities that generate substantial profits but pose significant risks to economic stability. The 2008 financial crisis was a direct consequence of this deregulated environment, with financial institutions engaging in risky lending practices that led to economic collapse and widespread hardship.

One of the most profound impacts of deregulation is the rise of tax havens, which have enabled corporations and high-net-worth individuals to avoid their fair share of taxation. These tax havens—often small jurisdictions with low or no corporate taxes—allow businesses to shift profits offshore, depriving governments of critical revenue needed to fund public services and infrastructure. Companies like Apple, Google, and Amazon have come under scrutiny for using complex financial structures to minimise their tax liabilities, legally exploiting gaps in international tax frameworks.

One of the most striking revelations of global tax evasion came with the Panama Papers leak in 2016, which exposed how the world's elite—corporations, politicians, celebrities, and business leaders—used offshore tax havens to hide vast amounts of wealth. The 11.5 million leaked documents from the Panamanian law firm Mossack Fonseca provided undeniable proof of large-scale financial secrecy and tax avoidance schemes that deprived governments of much-needed revenue.

The fallout was immediate and widespread. Politicians and business leaders faced public outrage, resignations, and legal scrutiny, with Iceland's Prime Minister stepping down and various governments launching investigations. More importantly, the revelations deepened public distrust in financial institutions and political elites, reinforcing the belief that the wealthy play by an entirely different set of rules. The Panama Papers did not just expose corruption; they fuelled populist sentiment, stoked anger against economic inequity, and intensified calls for tax reform and financial transparency. Yet, despite the shockwaves, meaningful change has been slow, with many of the same loopholes still being exploited today.

In addition to tax avoidance, deregulation has facilitated wealth concentration by allowing the erosion of labour protections. As governments have rolled back laws that safeguard workers' rights, businesses have been able to suppress wages, undermine unions, and create precarious working conditions. This has resulted in stagnant income growth for workers, even as corporate profits continue to soar.

Policy failures have also exacerbated wealth concentration, as governments often prioritise economic growth metrics over social welfare and equitable wealth distribution. Political influence wielded by wealthy individuals and corporate lobbyists has resulted in tax cuts for the rich, deregulation of financial markets, and weakened labour protections. The 2008 financial crisis, for example, highlighted the consequences of lax regulatory frameworks that prioritised short-term profits over economic stability, leading to job losses and economic hardship for millions while banks and corporations received government bailouts.

Moreover, the influence of money in politics has led to policies that disproportionately benefit the wealthy. Political donations and lobbying efforts have allowed corporations to shape regulations in their favour, further entrenching economic disparities. This influence often manifests in the form of tax breaks, subsidies, and other incentives that primarily benefit large businesses rather than the broader public.

Furthermore, many countries have adopted austerity measures as a response to economic crises, cutting essential public services while failing to address the underlying structural inequalities. These policy choices have widened the gap between the wealthy and the working class, eroding trust in public institutions and increasing social unrest.

The consequences of these policy failures are evident in the growing wealth disparity across the globe. In the United States, for instance, the top 1% of earners control more wealth than the entire middle class combined. In the UK, wealth inequality continues to rise despite economic growth, with stagnant wages and rising living costs squeezing lower-income households.

The Social and Economic Impacts of Policy Failures

The impact of deregulation and policy failures extends beyond economic inequality. Societal structures are increasingly strained as public services such as healthcare, education, and social security become underfunded due to the shrinking tax base. Wealth concentration also leads to increased political polarisation, social unrest, and a loss of trust in democratic institutions, as people feel excluded from the benefits of economic growth.

Additionally, environmental degradation has been exacerbated by deregulation. Without strict oversight, corporations prioritise profit over sustainability, leading to pollution, resource depletion, and climate change. The consequences of environmental damage disproportionately affect lower-income communities, further compounding social inequalities.

In many developing economies, deregulation has led to the exploitation of natural resources and labour, with foreign corporations extracting wealth without adequately investing in local communities. This has left many countries dependent on volatile global markets, unable to develop sustainable economies that benefit their populations.

Addressing the Issue

Addressing the issues arising from deregulation, tax havens, and policy failures requires a multifaceted approach. Governments must adopt stronger regulatory frameworks that prioritise fair competition, workers' rights, and environmental sustainability. Stricter enforcement of tax laws, coupled with international cooperation to curb tax avoidance, is essential to ensure corporations and the ultra-wealthy contribute their fair share.

Introducing progressive taxation policies, such as wealth taxes and financial transaction taxes, can help redistribute wealth more equitably. Additionally, governments should invest in social programmes, education, and infrastructure to create opportunities for economic mobility and reduce dependency on short-term corporate growth strategies.

Conclusion

Deregulation, tax havens, and policy failures have all played a crucial role in the concentration of wealth in the 21st century. These systemic issues have not only contributed to economic inequality but have also weakened social cohesion and public trust in institutions. Addressing these challenges requires bold policy changes, greater corporate accountability, and a renewed focus on economic justice to ensure a fairer distribution of wealth and opportunities for all. Without such measures, the widening gap between the wealthy elite and the rest of society will continue to threaten economic stability and social harmony.

Part II
The Societal Consequences of Wealth Inequity

Introduction

Wealth inequity is seldom a purely economic concern, as it reshapes the very fabric of societies, sowing discord and altering political landscapes in profound ways. In the late twentieth and early twenty-first centuries, globalization, technological acceleration, and evolving political alliances have all contributed to the rise of a new form of wealth disparity. This disparity extends well beyond individual bank accounts, manifesting instead in systemic imbalances that touch nearly every aspect of public life—from healthcare provision and educational opportunities to civic participation and cultural identity.

As wealth concentrates in fewer hands, the foundations of social cohesion begin to tremble. Communities once bound by shared economic experiences become fragmented, with the ultra-wealthy increasingly secluded in enclaves protected by private security and exclusive institutions, while struggling populations attempt to navigate precarious job markets and dwindling public services. The resulting tensions often mutate into larger-scale upheavals, whether in the form of populist uprisings, extremist movements, or widespread social unrest.

In this second part of our exploration of wealth inequity, we turn our attention to the societal consequences of these economic imbalances. We begin by examining geopolitical upheaval, a category encompassing everything from shifting alliances and regional conflicts to large-scale migrations triggered by economic desperation. We then delve into political disruptions in modern democracies, highlighting how wealth disparities can fuel polarization and pave the way for political outsiders—or populists— to rise to power by exploiting legitimate grievances.

Moving forward, we investigate the surge of far-right movements across Europe, the Americas, and other regions, noting that many of these groups have harnessed economic anxieties to bolster nationalist, xenophobic, or authoritarian agendas. Finally, we tie these modern developments to a broader historical context, showing how extreme inequality has repeatedly set the stage for revolutions and rebellions. From the French Revolution to the Bolshevik uprising, history provides telling cautionary tales about what can happen when inequity festers.

By surveying these manifestations of social unrest, we gain a clearer understanding of why wealth inequity constitutes a pressing threat not only to those on the lower rungs of the economic ladder but also to the stability of entire nations. Far from being an isolated phenomenon, modern inequalities are deeply interwoven with political, cultural, and historical forces. If allowed to intensify unchecked, they have the potential to unravel existing power structures, upend international alliances, and inaugurate periods of profound, often violent, transformation. The pages that follow aim to illuminate the risks, the patterns, and the warning signs in an attempt to encourage a nuanced discussion about how best to address one of the twenty-first century's most urgent challenges.

Geopolitical Upheaval

Economic Drivers of Global Tension

The most visible manifestation of wealth inequity on the global stage lies in stark economic contrasts between nations. While some countries enjoy advanced technology sectors, robust infrastructure, and high standards of living, others struggle with crippling debt, outdated industries, and insufficient healthcare systems. This disparity fuels migrations, trade imbalances, and, more profoundly, a sense of injustice and resentment. Wealth inequity does not only separate individuals within nations; it also places entire regions at odds, creating geopolitical fault lines that can escalate into conflict.

One of the most salient examples in recent decades is the mass migration from poorer regions in Africa, Latin America, and the Middle East to wealthier areas such as Europe and North America. Though these migrations are often framed as cultural or security issues, economic desperation and the search for better opportunities lie at the heart of such movements. Refugees and economic migrants frequently leave their homes because local economies offer no stable paths forward, and wealth is concentrated in the hands of a narrow elite.

When large numbers of people move across borders, the receiving countries face socioeconomic pressures, prompting political debates that can become flashpoints in elections. Politicians may scapegoat migrants for economic woes, even though the root cause is often broader structural inequality on a global scale.

This kind of displacement also creates ripple effects in international relations. Countries with high rates of emigration lose portions of their most industrious or educated citizens, further undermining their potential for economic growth and reinforcing cycles of poverty. Meanwhile, wealthier nations grapple with integration challenges, often devising policies that oscillate between humanitarian concern and stringent border controls. The tension between these impulses can fuel populist rhetoric and sharpen divides within domestic politics, revealing just how deeply wealth inequity influences geopolitical fault lines.

Resource Competition and Neo-Colonial Dynamics

Wealth inequity is also closely bound to resource competition. Nations endowed with abundant natural resources—oil, gas, precious minerals, or fertile farmland—can find themselves locked in exploitative relationships with more powerful countries or multinational corporations. In many instances, local populations see little benefit from resource extraction, as profits flow to foreign or elite interests. This dynamic, often termed a "neo-colonial" relationship, can breed resentment and anti-foreign sentiment, sometimes erupting into violence or protracted civil conflicts.

A clear illustration is the Niger Delta in Nigeria, where vast oil reserves have drawn multinational oil companies for decades.

Despite the wealth generated, local communities suffer from environmental degradation, poor infrastructure, and negligible economic benefits. Similar patterns have occurred in parts of the Middle East, Central Asia, and South America. The resulting unrest has not only destabilized local governments but has also led to increased militarization, further entrenching power imbalances and stifling development.

At a broader level, these extractive relationships reinforce global wealth disparities, as corporate executives and shareholders—often based in wealthy nations—accumulate massive profits, while locals remain impoverished. The ensuing anger can target both domestic elites, seen as collaborators, and foreign entities, viewed as imperialistic exploiters. Ultimately, these tensions can spiral into regional conflicts or terrorist insurgencies, thereby contributing to international instability.

Technological Shifts and the New Global Order

The rapid development of technology, particularly the digital revolution, has introduced another layer to geopolitical upheaval. On one hand, technology promises the democratization of information, improved connectivity, and new business opportunities. On the other hand, it can deepen wealth inequity by bestowing disproportionate advantages upon those with access to digital infrastructure, education, and capital.

Countries with thriving tech sectors, such as the United States, China, parts of Europe, and increasingly India, have rapidly modernized their economies, creating fresh classes of billionaires and global corporations. In contrast, many developing nations lack the resources to invest significantly in education, high-speed internet, or research and development. This digital divide can be seen as a modern extension of historical inequities, wherein wealthy nations remain at the forefront of innovation while poorer regions lag behind, reliant on imported goods, technology, and expertise.

This form of economic globalization has also triggered a new wave of competition between major powers. The United States and China, for instance, vie for influence through technological alliances and trade agreements, using their economic leverage to shape global norms. Smaller or less developed countries find themselves in precarious positions, forced to align with one bloc or risk being shut out of vital economic networks. The entire landscape of international relations is thus recalibrated, again underscoring how wealth inequity sets the stage for geopolitical battles that affect millions of people.

Climate Change as an Accelerant

Climate change, often overlooked in discussions of wealth inequity, is an accelerant of existing geopolitical tensions. Nations that lack the financial and technological means to adapt to rising sea levels, extreme weather events, and resource scarcity frequently bear the brunt of environmental disasters. Wealthy countries can build flood defenses, shift agricultural zones, or invest in new energy infrastructure, whereas poorer nations remain vulnerable to crop failures, famine, and destructive storms.

The resulting crises lead to internal displacement, food insecurity, and, in some cases, civil strife or cross-border conflicts. Entire regions may become uninhabitable, triggering migratory movements and political discord. Climate-induced disasters also stretch governmental budgets, leaving less room for public spending on education or healthcare, thereby aggravating wealth inequities at a domestic level.

At the international level, disputes over water rights or fishing grounds can escalate quickly, reflecting the deeper economic and political schisms that define our era. Thus, climate change acts as a force multiplier, exacerbating existing inequalities and animating fresh waves of migration and political friction. When combined with other facets of global wealth disparity—such as resource competition, technological gaps, and historical patterns of exploitation—climate stressors highlight the fragility of international systems.

Shifting Alliances and Populist Diplomacy

Geo-political upheaval driven by wealth inequity also reconfigures alliances. Traditional institutions like the European Union or NATO find themselves under strain when member states feel short-changed by existing economic arrangements. Populist governments may campaign on promises to renegotiate trade deals or withdraw from certain treaties, arguing that these agreements benefit an out-of-touch elite at the expense of ordinary people. Brexit stands as a prime example: while the decision to leave the EU was motivated by multiple factors, concerns about economic sovereignty, migration, and dissatisfaction with perceived "elites" in Brussels all played central roles.

Such renegotiations or withdrawals can unsettle established regional balances, encouraging other states to reassess their commitments or follow suit. This domino effect contributes to an atmosphere of uncertainty, impacting global markets, diplomatic relations, and collective efforts on issues such as security or environmental protection. In the background, the persistent drumbeat of inequality gives populist leaders both their rallying cry and their justification for sweeping changes—often with repercussions that extend far beyond their national borders.

Political Disruptions

The Erosion of the Political Center

A notable consequence of wealth inequity is the polarization of political landscapes, with moderate voices losing ground to those at the extremes. As middle-class voters feel their standard of living is threatened and working-class communities experience long-term decline, trust in established political parties diminishes. The perceived failure of centrist politicians to address rising living costs, precarious employment, and shrinking public services drives many toward radical alternatives, whether on the left or the right.

In Europe, the once-stable arrangement between center-left and center-right parties has been shattered in several countries. France witnessed the collapse of its traditional two-party system, giving way to Emmanuel Macron's *En Marche* on one side and Marine Le Pen's National Rally on the other. In Spain, the rise of Podemos on the left and Vox on the right illustrates the fragmentation of a political arena once dominated by the Socialists and the Popular Party. In each case, underlying economic grievances have fueled dissatisfaction, pushing voters to seek more radical or populist options.

As the political center erodes, policymaking becomes more volatile. Coalitions are harder to forge, and governments often lack stable majorities, leading to indecision on critical matters like healthcare, immigration, and economic reforms. This deadlock can breed further disillusionment, perpetuating a cycle wherein voters lurch between extremes in search of meaningful change.

The Rise of Populist Outsiders

Populism thrives in conditions of inequality and social distress. Populist leaders often position themselves as defenders of the "common people" against a corrupt or indifferent elite. They exploit genuine grievances tied to wage stagnation, job insecurity, and public spending cuts. By channeling anger toward convenient scapegoats—immigrants, international institutions, or minority groups—these politicians construct a narrative that resonates with those who feel alienated from traditional politics.

The election of Donald Trump in the United States in 2016 stands out as a prime example. Trump's campaign drew heavily on the discontent of communities affected by deindustrialization, promising to bring back manufacturing jobs and renegotiate trade deals. His rhetoric targeted both Washington elites and foreign nations, painting them as conspirators against "everyday Americans." In Europe, similarly styled politicians such as Viktor Orbán in Hungary, Matteo Salvini in Italy, and Marine Le Pen in France have harnessed parallel sentiments, pledging to protect national interests from globalist agendas.

In his return to office in 2025, Trump's election has been marked by a series of swift and decisive policy actions, fundamentally reshaping the direction of the federal government. His administration wasted no time in overturning key policies from the previous administration, reinforcing his vision of nationalism, deregulation, and economic restructuring.

One of Trump's most immediate priorities has been rolling back financial regulations that had been put in place after the 2008 financial crisis. His administration swiftly suspended the activities of the Consumer Financial Protection Bureau (CFPB), an agency created to oversee financial institutions and protect consumers from predatory lending practices. This move, while celebrated by Wall Street and corporate interests, has sparked concerns among economists and consumer rights advocates who fear a return to reckless financial behavior that could once again destabilize markets. Trump also signed executive orders reducing oversight on banks and hedge funds, arguing that deregulation would stimulate economic growth and increase lending to businesses. Critics, however, warn that such measures primarily benefit the financial elite and could lead to increased economic disparity.

In an unprecedented move, Trump directed federal agencies to dismiss all probationary employees, leading to massive reductions in the federal workforce. Estimates suggest that over 200,000 government employees could be affected, impacting agencies across health, environmental regulation, and public services. This action aligns with Trump's long-standing promise to "drain the swamp" by reducing the size of government, but it has been met with resistance from unions, public service organizations, and civil rights groups, who argue that such large-scale dismissals will weaken institutional knowledge and disrupt essential services.

Wealth Inequity and the Rise of Oligarchy

As corporate influence expands under Trump's administration, concerns about wealth inequity have deepened. His economic policies—focused on cutting corporate taxes, reducing capital gains taxes, and eliminating regulatory barriers—have disproportionately benefited the wealthiest Americans, exacerbating existing disparities. The first months of his presidency have seen billionaires and major business figures gain even greater influence in policymaking, with several high-profile corporate executives appointed to key advisory positions.

Trump's continued alignment with figures such as Elon Musk, Peter Thiel, and hedge fund executives has further reinforced a governance model that places economic power in the hands of a few. Many analysts argue that the U.S. is evolving into an oligarchy, where financial elites wield significant influence over policy decisions. Critics point to the administration's tax policies, which have prioritized corporate interests over social programs, as evidence of this shift. The stock market has soared under Trump's leadership, driven largely by tax cuts and deregulation, but wages for average workers remain stagnant, and income inequality continues to grow.

Foreign Policy and Trade Wars

Trump's return to office has also brought renewed trade tensions with China and the European Union. In an effort to "bring back American jobs," he has imposed new tariffs on Chinese imports, a move that has sparked retaliatory measures from Beijing. This economic nationalism, while appealing to Trump's base, has drawn criticism from trade experts who warn of increased costs for American consumers and potential job losses in industries dependent on global supply chains.

Additionally, Trump has reasserted his stance on NATO, demanding that European allies increase their financial contributions to defense spending or risk reduced U.S. support. This has strained relationships with key allies and raised concerns about the stability of global security agreements. Meanwhile, Trump's administration has strengthened ties with autocratic leaders, further signaling a shift away from traditional diplomatic norms.

The Erosion of Democratic Norms

This second term has also raised alarms about the erosion of democratic institutions. His administration has continued to challenge the legitimacy of media organizations critical of his policies, often dismissing them as "fake news" while favoring outlets that align with his ideological stance. There have been renewed efforts to weaken federal oversight agencies, particularly those responsible for investigating executive branch misconduct.

Moreover, Trump has advocated for changes to electoral laws that critics argue could suppress voter participation. His administration has pushed for stricter voting regulations under the guise of preventing fraud, despite the lack of evidence supporting widespread election fraud claims. Civil rights groups have condemned these efforts, arguing that they disproportionately affect minority and low-income voters.

Public Reaction and Political Landscape

Public response to Trump's presidency has been deeply polarized. His supporters view his actions as a necessary correction to years of establishment politics, praising his unapologetic approach to governance. To them, his presidency represents a return to American strength, economic growth, and a rejection of globalist influences.

However, opposition to Trump has been equally fierce. Protests have erupted across major cities, with demonstrators calling for economic justice, climate action, and protections for marginalized communities. The Democratic Party, still reeling from its 2024 electoral loss, has struggled to unify around a clear strategy to counter Trump's policies.

Labor unions, civil rights organizations, and consumer advocacy groups have also mobilized, warning that Trump's policies are accelerating wealth inequality and undermining democratic principles. Calls for increased taxation on the wealthy, stronger labor protections, and campaign finance reform have grown louder, though legislative gridlock has prevented meaningful progress in these areas.

Looking Ahead

As Trump's second term unfolds, the long-term consequences of his policies remain uncertain. While his administration has bolstered corporate profits and reasserted American nationalism, it has also widened the wealth gap and intensified social and political divisions. The rise of oligarchy in the United States—where economic elites hold disproportionate influence over policy—poses a significant challenge to the principles of democracy and economic fairness.

The question now is whether the U.S. will continue on this path of deepening wealth inequality or whether public pressure will force a re-evaluation of economic and political priorities. History has shown that when economic disparity reaches unsustainable levels, upheaval becomes inevitable. The first months of Trump's presidency have set the stage for a critical period of reckoning—one that will determine the future of wealth distribution, governance, and democracy in America.

Eroding Trust in Institutions

Political disruptions are inseparable from a broader collapse in public trust toward institutions, including parliament, judiciary systems, the media, and even scientific bodies. As societies become more unequal, many perceive that these institutions serve elite interests rather than the common good. This erosion of trust is not restricted to a single political ideology; both left-wing and right-wing movements highlight institutional biases.

Media conglomerates often face criticism for being part of an establishment that fails to question corporate or governmental overreach. Central banks and regulatory agencies are likewise accused of catering to financial elites, particularly after the 2008 global financial crisis, when banks received massive bailouts even as ordinary families lost their homes. Educational institutions— traditionally viewed as ladders to upward mobility—are increasingly seen as bastions of privilege, given the soaring costs of higher education and the advantage that wealthier students enjoy in admissions processes.

The digital revolution has also transformed how people receive and interpret information. Conspiracy theories and "fake news" proliferate across social media, exacerbating distrust in mainstream narratives. In a climate where official sources are suspect, alternative media voices gain traction by claiming to offer unfiltered "truths." This can rapidly become dangerous, as extremist ideologies flourish in echo chambers, turning frustration at inequality into a breeding ground for radical or violent action.

The Role of Corruption and Cronyism

As political systems grow more polarized and institutions lose credibility, corruption and cronyism often intensify, further entrenching wealth inequity. Corporate lobbying, private campaign financing, and revolving-door appointments between government and industry have become hallmarks of modern politics. These practices reinforce the perception that the system is rigged, particularly when policies enacted appear to disproportionately benefit large corporations or high-net-worth individuals.

In many countries, the political class is seen as out of touch with ordinary struggles. Elected officials may enjoy robust pensions, generous healthcare plans, and personal connections to business tycoons, all of which insulate them from the economic realities of their constituents. This disconnect widens the gulf between government and the governed, feeding cynicism and its counterpart: the search for anti-establishment figures who promise radical reforms.

From Latin America to Eastern Europe, high-profile corruption scandals have brought down governments and triggered mass protests. In Brazil, the "Operation Car Wash" investigation exposed a vast network of corporate and political bribery, eroding trust in parties across the ideological spectrum. In Eastern Europe, oligarchic interests often dominate political spheres, ensuring that legislation protects their financial empires while public services languish. The end result is an electorate quick to anger, ready to embrace strongmen who pledge to root out corruption—only to discover later that these leaders often perpetuate or worsen the problem.

Far-Right Movements

Exploiting Economic Anxiety

Far-right movements have experienced a resurgence across multiple continents, thriving on economic anxieties that stem directly from wealth inequity. When people perceive their livelihoods to be threatened—be it due to global competition, immigration, or technological displacement—they can become more receptive to extremist narratives. Far-right groups often vilify ethnic minorities, immigrants, or religious communities, claiming that these groups are "stealing" jobs or resources from the native population.

Such narratives simplify complex economic realities. Instead of addressing systemic issues, like inadequate labor protections or regressive tax structures, far-right movements direct ire toward the most visible "other." This strategy resonates especially in regions that have undergone deindustrialization or suffered from chronic underinvestment, where residents feel forgotten by metropolitan elites. The scapegoating process fosters social division and distracts from the true drivers of inequity—whether corporate malfeasance, automation, or international trade imbalances.

Nationalism and the Promise of "Taking Back Control"

Far-right ideologies tend to frame their proposals as a means to "take back control." This involves reasserting national sovereignty, implementing draconian immigration policies, and sometimes even withdrawing from international alliances or treaties. The subtext often includes the idea that the nation, once pure and prosperous, has fallen under the sway of corrupt elites or foreign influences that weaken its moral and economic fabric.

Brexit provided a modern-day illustration of this rhetoric. Although not every Leave supporter was far-right, the campaign frequently invoked the concept of reclaiming British independence—"taking back control"—from European technocrats. This message found fertile ground among voters who felt sidelined by globalization and left behind by Britain's metropolitan hubs. Politicians capitalized on socio-economic disparities between prosperous urban centers like London and struggling post-industrial regions, reinforcing the narrative that escaping the European Union would restore fairness and prosperity.

Elsewhere, far-right factions have demanded the deportation of undocumented migrants, the closure of borders, or the renunciation of international human rights agreements. While such policies are often framed as protective measures, they rarely address the core economic imbalances that fuel social discontent. In many cases, they simply channel popular anger away from the structural roots of wealth inequity and toward convenient targets.

Militarization and Paramilitary Groups

In the most extreme scenarios, far-right movements adopt militaristic or paramilitary strategies, posing a direct threat to social stability and democratic norms. History shows that when inequity reaches a boiling point, disenfranchised individuals are sometimes drawn to groups that offer a sense of purpose, unity, or belonging— often accompanied by violent rhetoric or actions. These groups can gain traction by portraying themselves as guardians against perceived enemies, ranging from religious minorities to "globalist" conspirators.

Modern examples include militia movements in the United States, some of which have roots in rural areas affected by industrial decline or economic stagnation. In Europe, neo-Nazi or ultranationalist gangs have carried out hate crimes against immigrant communities, perceiving them as both cultural and economic threats. The internet further facilitates these groups' recruitment efforts, allowing them to spread propaganda and organize events across borders.

Such militarization tears at the social fabric, leading to heightened tensions between different communities. In divided societies, violence can flare up swiftly, sometimes with deadly consequences. Governments face the challenge of balancing civil liberties with the need to curb extremist groups—a task complicated by the fact that some far-right ideologies overlap with mainstream political rhetoric, making them harder to isolate or delegitimize.

Political Mainstreaming

A critical feature of the current far-right wave is how often these movements manage to infiltrate mainstream politics. Unlike in past decades, when overtly neo-fascist or ultra-nationalist rhetoric was widely condemned, today many far-right talking points have been softened or repackaged to appeal to a broader swath of voters. Themes like "law and order," "cultural preservation," or "national sovereignty" can resonate with those who are not strictly far-right but are disillusioned with moderate politicians.

Once elected, far-right leaders can reshape institutions to cement their power. They might curtail press freedoms, politicize the judiciary, or weaken legislative checks and balances, all under the guise of fulfilling the people's will. As a result, democratic norms erode, and societies become more receptive to authoritarian measures, particularly when cloaked in nationalist rhetoric. This process can be observed in countries such as Hungary and Poland, where right-wing governments have passed legislation limiting judicial independence and tightening state control over media.

Donald Trump's appointments to the U.S. Supreme Court marked one of the most consequential shifts in American judicial history, solidifying a conservative majority that would shape legal precedent for generations. By appointing three justices—Neil Gorsuch, Brett Kavanaugh, and Amy Coney Barrett—Trump, with the backing of Senate Republicans, strategically reshaped the court to favor corporate interests, deregulation, and the rollback of progressive policies. The rushed confirmation of Barrett just days before the 2020 presidential election, despite Republicans having previously blocked a nomination in an election year under Obama, exposed the stark hypocrisy and manipulation of judicial appointments for political gain.

These appointments underscored how governments can subvert democracy by stacking the judiciary with ideological allies, ensuring that judicial decisions align with political objectives rather than the broader public interest. The Supreme Court, intended as an impartial arbiter of justice, has instead become a tool of power consolidation, where legal rulings increasingly reflect partisan priorities rather than constitutional fairness. This shift highlights the broader global trend of governments using judicial appointments to entrench their influence and insulate themselves from democratic accountability.

Mainstreaming also occurs through coalition governance. In some parliamentary systems, traditional conservative parties have formed alliances with far-right factions to secure majorities. Over time, the ideological lines blur, and previously extreme ideas gain legitimacy through proximity to established governing bodies. This incremental acceptance of far-right beliefs underscores how wealth inequity fuels a broader shift in political discourse, as frustration and fear overshadow rational policy debates about the economy's structural flaws.

Backlash and Counter-Movements

While far-right movements have gained momentum, they invariably provoke counter-movements among citizens alarmed by xenophobia, racism, or authoritarian tactics. Grassroots organizations, civil rights groups, and leftist coalitions rally around causes such as social justice, inclusion, and the protection of democratic institutions. Many younger voters, in particular, express deep concern about the normalization of far-right views, seeing them as an affront to multicultural values and human rights.

This backlash can manifest in protests, social media campaigns, and electoral strategies aimed at mobilizing voter turnout. In some cases, these efforts succeed in stalling or reversing far-right advances. However, the broader societal fissures remain unless the root causes—economic desperation, social marginalization, and widening inequality—are addressed comprehensively.

Historical Echoes of Revolutions

The French Revolution: A Stark Warning

Few historical events highlight the societal consequences of wealth inequity more powerfully than the French Revolution. In the decades leading up to 1789, France's Ancien Régime was marked by severe economic stratification. The nobility and clergy enjoyed vast privileges and often paid minimal taxes, leaving the brunt of the tax burden on the Third Estate—peasants, laborers, and the burgeoning bourgeoisie. Widespread crop failures, heavy state debts, and the conspicuous consumption of the royal court fueled public outrage.

When Parisians stormed the Bastille, they not only overthrew a symbol of royal authority but also ignited a continent-wide wave of transformation. The Revolution unleashed fervent calls for liberty, equality, and fraternity, encapsulating the hope that centuries of aristocratic dominance could finally be upended. Yet this period also demonstrated how quickly revolutionary ideals can devolve into violence and factional strife. The Reign of Terror, led by the Jacobins, saw thousands executed in a climate of suspicion and paranoia. Eventually, Napoleon Bonaparte seized power, trading revolutionary chaos for imperial ambition.

The French Revolution thus provides a nuanced lesson. On one hand, it illustrates that extreme wealth inequity can culminate in sudden upheaval, toppling once-untouchable elites. On the other hand, it warns that revolutions themselves can become volatile and destructive, sometimes failing to achieve the egalitarian outcomes that inspired them in the first place.

The Russian Revolutions: Economic Desperation and Ideological Ferment

A second instructive example is the sequence of Russian Revolutions in the early twentieth century, culminating in the Bolshevik Revolution of 1917. Tsarist Russia was a vast empire with profound social and economic divisions. A small aristocracy owned much of the land, while peasants lived in near-feudal conditions, burdened by heavy rents and taxes. Industrial workers in urban centers faced harsh labor conditions, low wages, and little representation.

The First World War exacerbated these inequities, as soldiers from peasant backgrounds suffered horrifying casualties while the aristocracy largely avoided the front lines. Food shortages in the cities became acute, and strikes and protests proliferated. The February Revolution of 1917 forced Tsar Nicholas II to abdicate, replacing the autocracy with a provisional government. Yet this new regime did not address the pressing issues of land reform and food distribution fast enough, paving the way for the Bolsheviks—led by Vladimir Lenin—to seize power in the October Revolution.

Like the French Revolution, the Russian case illuminates the close relationship between extreme wealth inequity and political upheaval. However, the Bolshevik victory also teaches a crucial lesson about the role of ideology. Marxist ideas found fertile ground in a populace exhausted by war and social injustice. The Revolution promised to redistribute land and wealth, appealing to the desperate desire for radical change. But the subsequent establishment of a one-party state under Lenin and later Stalin would introduce its own brand of oppression, including famines, purges, and gulags. This trajectory underscores that while revolutions may start with promises of equality, they can quickly lapse into authoritarianism if checks and balances are absent.

Colonial Revolutions: The Struggle Against Imperial Wealth Extraction

Beyond the European context, decolonization movements provide another lens for understanding how entrenched inequity can spark mass rebellion. Throughout the eighteenth, nineteenth, and twentieth centuries, European powers extracted massive wealth from colonies in Africa, Asia, and the Americas, enriching domestic elites while subjecting colonized populations to exploitation and subjugation. Over time, colonial subjects, educated in Western political thought yet denied its benefits, organized themselves for independence.

These struggles ranged from the largely peaceful (such as India's nonviolent resistance under Mahatma Gandhi) to the brutally violent (as in Algeria's war for independence from France). In each case, the fundamental grievance was the same: colonial rule perpetuated a stark imbalance of wealth and power, violating the principles of self-determination and fairness. While many colonies eventually achieved independence, the legacies of colonial exploitation often lingered in the form of corrupt local elites, neo-colonial economic structures, or drawn-out civil wars.

The history of Ireland's struggle against British rule is a stark example of colonial exploitation and the societal fractures that emerge from systemic inequity. The Great Famine (1845–1852) remains one of the most tragic consequences of colonial mismanagement, where British policies exacerbated the suffering of the Irish people, leading to mass starvation, death, and emigration. While Ireland was part of the United Kingdom at the time, the British government's response—favoring economic dogma over humanitarian relief—deepened resentment and fueled nationalist movements that would eventually drive the push for independence.

This legacy of inequity persisted into the twentieth century, culminating in the partition of Ireland and the creation of Northern Ireland, where economic disparity and sectarian divisions were entrenched. British governance reinforced inequality, as political and economic power remained concentrated among the Protestant elite, leaving Catholic communities disenfranchised. Decades of discrimination in housing, employment, and civil rights led to the outbreak of The Troubles (1960s–1998), a conflict rooted in colonial history but exacerbated by economic inequality and systemic exclusion. The Good Friday Agreement (1998) sought to address these divides, but even in modern times, Brexit has reignited tensions, demonstrating that the effects of colonial rule and economic disparity continue to shape political realities in the region.

Lessons from Minor Uprisings and Labor Movements

Larger-scale revolutions draw the most historical attention, but smaller uprisings and labor movements offer valuable insights into how wealth inequity shapes collective action. Throughout the nineteenth and early twentieth centuries, Europe and North America witnessed countless strikes, factory occupations, and demonstrations as workers fought for better wages, safer conditions, and shorter working hours. These movements rarely sought to overthrow governments outright, but they fundamentally challenged the prevailing economic order by asserting labor rights.

From the Chartist movement in Britain to the rise of syndicalism in France and anarchism in Spain, myriad ideologies coalesced around the struggle against wealth concentration. Even when these movements did not seize political power, they often compelled employers and governments to concede reforms: legalizing trade unions, establishing minimum wage laws, or enacting social welfare programs. This incremental progress served as a pressure valve, mitigating the worst excesses of inequality and thereby postponing or averting more sweeping revolutions.

Modern parallels exist in the form of teachers' strikes, healthcare worker protests, and gig economy demonstrations. Although these contemporary movements may lack the revolutionary fervor of historical uprisings, they are united by the same logic: wealth inequity is unsustainable, and workers will organize and protest if their livelihoods and dignity are repeatedly undermined.

The Fragility of Revolutions and the Cycle of Inequity

The historical record also shows that revolutions, even when successful in the short term, can gradually reproduce new forms of inequity. Power vacuums, factional infighting, and opportunistic leadership often derail the pursuit of egalitarian ideals. Over time, new elites emerge—whether in the form of military dictatorships, one-party states, or oligarchic cliques—who then concentrate wealth and influence in their own hands.

This cyclical nature underscores a crucial point: the societal consequences of wealth inequity are not resolved simply by toppling existing regimes. Sustainable change requires robust institutions, transparent governance, and mechanisms for ongoing public participation. Otherwise, the same patterns of exploitation and oppression may reassert themselves, albeit under different banners.

Conclusion: A Trembling Balance

The societal consequences of wealth inequity are far-reaching, woven through the fabric of geopolitical alliances, domestic political spheres, far-right resurgence, and historical patterns of rebellion. Whether we examine the migrations prompted by global economic disparities, the populist fervor sweeping across democratic nations, the extremist ideologies taking root in disenfranchised communities, or the revolutionary upheavals etched into history, a consistent thread emerges: where wealth is heavily concentrated, social unrest grows, and the very structures that once seemed impervious—governments, institutions, even entire empires—begin to quake.

Geopolitical upheaval shows that inequities between nations can spark migratory pressures, border tensions, and regional conflicts, especially when natural resources are unevenly distributed or climate change intensifies competition for habitable land.

Meanwhile, political disruptions demonstrate how concentrated wealth undermines democratic norms, leading voters to embrace populist leaders who promise to redress perceived injustices but often perpetuate division. The far-right movements that have recently gained traction exploit economic grievances by blaming outsiders, reinforcing narratives that distract from systemic issues.

Finally, historical revolutions provide vivid cautionary tales: from France to Russia, from the colonial world to myriad smaller labor rebellions, societies have repeatedly risen against entrenched elites, sometimes achieving great transformations, sometimes merely trading one oppressive structure for another.

Ultimately, this second part of our exploration underlines a fundamental fact: wealth inequity is not a static or isolated condition. It is a dynamic force that reshapes political alliances, stokes ideological fervor, and rekindles age-old debates about justice and legitimacy. Societies organized around vast imbalances of power and resources become inherently fragile, vulnerable to sudden upheavals that can rewrite national borders, topple governments, or spark seemingly endless cycles of violence.

In confronting this reality, we are forced to recognize that policies addressing wealth inequity are not merely acts of redistribution—they are acts of social preservation. They are the means by which societies can avert the worst forms of conflict and work toward a more stable, equitable future.

So, in Part Two, I have tried to illustrate how these tensions manifest and offer a lens through which to view the dangers of ignoring the economic fault lines that run beneath our political and social structures. As we progress to further sections, I will examine more specific pathways through which societies might address wealth disparities, seeking reforms that could temper the fractures outlined here. While the challenges are daunting, history also shows that transformation is not only possible—it is inevitable when the collective will demands it. The question remains whether these transformations will be steered by proactive measures or forced upon us by crisis and conflict.

.

Part III
When the Pitchforks Come

Introduction

As the global wealth gap widens and social unrest simmers just beneath the surface, it becomes increasingly plausible that the societal fabric might fray under the weight of inequality. In the earlier sections of this book, I have briefly charted the landscape of wealth disparity, examining how economic and political systems converge to create a precarious balance for billions of people. We have also explored the historical lessons of revolutions, recognizing that societies have, time and again, erupted into uprisings when inequity becomes intolerable.

In this third part, we turn our attention to the moment those simmering tensions boil over, focusing on the question of how a modern Western context might experience its own brand of "pitchforks." While some commentators argue that robust legal institutions and democratic norms make violent revolution unlikely, recent events—ranging from large-scale protests to insurrections at legislative buildings—suggest that Western societies are far from immune to disruptive upheaval.

In Chapter 7, *Revolution Reimagined: Scenarios for the West*, I will explore two parallel tracks: how a new wave of revolution could conceivably unfold along peaceful lines, harnessing the power of mass demonstrations, and how more violent insurgencies may emerge, propelled by anger and disillusionment. At the core of both possibilities lies technology: the catalysts of connectivity, social media, and digital platforms that simultaneously unite the disenfranchised and fragment public discourse.

In Chapter 8, *A Healthcare CEO's Assassination: The Breaking Point*, I shift the focus from the theoretical to the visceral. Through the lens of a fictional event—the murder of a high-profile healthcare executive—we see how public sentiment can erupt into a rallying cry, either casting the slain executive as a greedy symbol of corporate malpractice or a tragic victim of uncontrolled societal rage. The chapter scrutinizes how narratives can be spun, legitimized, or contested in the court of public opinion, revealing the delicate boundary between seeking justice and fueling vengeance.

Taken as a whole, in Part III, I hope to sketch a possible future in which the pitchforks—both literal and metaphorical—are no longer confined to historical memory. Whether the result is constructive transformation or destructive mayhem depends on a multitude of factors: leadership, public will, institutional resilience, and the interplay of technology with human agency. Yet beneath all these variables lurks the stubborn fact of inequity. Should our societies fail to address its root causes, the pitchforks may indeed come, challenging every assumption about stability, progress, and the sanctity of the current order.

Revolution Reimagined: Scenarios for the West

Peaceful Protests vs. Violent Uprisings

The Historical Context of Peaceful Resistance

Contemporary Western societies pride themselves on democratic traditions that, in theory at least, enable citizens to voice grievances without resorting to violence. The 20th century offers numerous examples of largely peaceful protest movements that enacted significant political change: Gandhi's nonviolent resistance in India, Martin Luther King Jr.'s civil rights marches in the United States, and mass protests in Eastern Europe leading up to the fall of the Berlin Wall. These instances of peaceful agitation demonstrate how collective action, rooted in moral conviction and broadly supported by the public, can indeed reshape entire nations.

In the current era, many activists continue to champion peaceful methods, inspired by the notion that violence begets violence. Large-scale marches, sit-ins, and public demonstrations remain key tactics for social movements. With the advent of social media, these actions can be organized at a speed and scale previously unimaginable. Videos of police crackdowns or corporate malfeasance can go viral, galvanizing popular support overnight. The Occupy Movement, which spread from Wall Street to cities around the world, exemplified how the simple act of gathering en masse in public spaces could spark a global conversation about financial injustice. Though it ultimately lacked a unified set of demands, Occupy's legacy endures in modern activist strategies, demonstrating that peaceful disruptions can influence discourse without spilling into outright chaos.

Why Violent Uprisings Still Occur

Despite the existence of democratic channels, violent uprisings remain a recurring feature in human history, including in relatively stable Western contexts. The reasons for this are manifold. First, democratic institutions may be perceived as corrupt, unresponsive, or captured by special interests—leading disillusioned individuals to deem peaceful methods ineffective. Second, the emotional volatility stoked by severe economic distress, racial injustices, or cultural clashes can provoke an urgent sense of desperation that pushes people toward confrontation. In such cases, acts of violence may be rationalized as "the language of the unheard," to borrow a phrase from Martin Luther King Jr.

Moreover, extremist ideologies often thrive in times of crisis. If wealth inequity triggers a profound sense of betrayal—where large segments of the population believe their aspirations have been systematically undermined by a self-serving elite—violence can become a tragically appealing outlet. Right-wing militias, left-wing insurrectionist groups, and anarchist collectives have all shown a willingness to exploit feelings of hopelessness, using them to recruit members and plan armed resistance. Even in countries with strict gun controls, the rise of 3D-printing technologies and black-market arms trades can place lethal tools into the hands of radicals willing to take up arms.

Hybrid Tactics and the Erosion of the Middle Ground

One emerging trend is the fusion of peaceful protest methods with sporadic, targeted acts of violence—what some analysts call "hybrid tactics." Demonstrations may begin peacefully, but a minority of participants can turn to property damage, looting, or direct attacks on law enforcement and political targets. This undermines the broader movement's legitimacy and can lead to public backlash, yet it also amplifies the sense of urgency and threat, potentially forcing authorities to negotiate more rapidly. Hybrid tactics become more likely in polarized environments, where moderate voices struggle to assert restraint over heterogeneous activist coalitions.

At the root of both purely peaceful and overtly violent forms of uprising is a search for recognition and redress. In a system riddled with wealth inequity, those on the losing end may conclude that institutional processes are either rigged or painfully slow. Whether they opt for nonviolent protest or armed revolt often depends on cultural traditions, the influence of ideological leaders, and the presence of repressive state responses. Ultimately, these pressures feed on each other, creating a self-reinforcing cycle: the more forcefully a government cracks down, the more likely some dissidents are to escalate their tactics, giving the authorities further justification for clampdowns.

The Role of Technology in Mobilising the Masses

Social Media as a Catalyst

The digital revolution has drastically altered the playing field for political engagement. Social media platforms—Twitter, Facebook, TikTok, Telegram, and others—enable activists to mobilize large crowds in a matter of hours. Hashtags become rallying cries, viral videos serve as the impetus for international solidarity campaigns, and fundraisers can accumulate thousands of dollars in minutes. This capacity to coordinate and amplify messages fuels both peaceful movements and extremist factions, leveling the informational playing field in ways that challenge traditional power structures.

During the Arab Spring, for instance, a single fruit vendor's self-immolation in Tunisia was swiftly broadcast online, igniting protests that toppled governments across North Africa and the Middle East. In Western contexts, Black Lives Matter started as a hashtag and erupted into a global phenomenon, revealing how social media could cultivate shared grievances into international activism almost overnight. For the disenfranchised, technology offers unprecedented means of exposure—no longer must one rely on mainstream media, which may be subject to editorial biases, to highlight injustice. Instead, anyone with a smartphone can document, publish, and organize.

The Dark Side of Digital Coordination

Yet the digital realm is not solely a bastion of empowerment. Algorithms designed to maximize engagement also thrive on polarizing content, pushing emotionally charged or divisive material to the forefront. Conspiracy theories can spread rapidly, and extremist groups recruit across private chat forums or encrypted messaging services. The same tools that support calls for justice can be weaponized to sow disinformation or galvanize violent cells.

Moreover, governments and corporations utilize advanced surveillance technologies to monitor and sometimes disrupt activist networks. Authoritarian regimes may deploy sophisticated spyware to track dissidents, while even democratic administrations engage in questionable data-gathering practices under the guise of national security. This environment fosters a digital arms race, where activists adapt by using secure platforms, code words, or ephemeral messaging, while states expand their surveillance capabilities, citing public safety concerns.

Cryptocurrency and the Funding of Revolts

One aspect often overlooked in discussions about modern uprisings is the financial dimension. Cryptocurrencies like Bitcoin and Ethereum provide a level of anonymity and bypass traditional banking systems, which can freeze accounts or monitor transactions to disrupt protest movements. If wealth inequality spurs a new wave of revolutionary fervor, activists could leverage decentralized finance (DeFi) to raise funds, purchase supplies, or even compensate participants without detection.

Such maneuvers complicate state efforts to contain unrest, as financial tracking has historically been a cornerstone of monitoring subversive activities. When capital can flow freely in and out of decentralized blockchain networks, the state's capacity to throttle a revolution's monetary lifeblood diminishes. Consequently, governments may move to restrict or ban digital currencies, framing them as enablers of organized crime or terrorist financing, even if their real concern is halting subversive political action.

Technological Countermeasures to Repressive Regimes

On the positive side, technology offers new avenues for nonviolent resistance in the face of repressive regimes. Secure messaging apps and decentralized social networks enable activists to coordinate strikes or mass demonstrations with fewer leaks or infiltration attempts by state security. Citizen journalism can document human rights abuses in real time, forcing political authorities to answer for violent crackdowns or extrajudicial arrests. In some cases, this scrutiny may deter governments from responding too harshly, lest they spark international condemnation or sanctions.

Further, open-source intelligence (OSINT) communities have emerged, allowing volunteer analysts to piece together evidence of wrongdoing—from identifying perpetrators of police brutality to pinpointing hidden supply lines for extremist factions. This democratization of data analysis puts new tools in the hands of average citizens, offering a form of watchdog oversight that was once impossible without institutional resources. While these developments certainly do not eliminate the risk of violent revolt, they demonstrate how technology shapes modern revolution, making it more dispersed, nimble, and responsive to real-time events.

From Warning to Reality: A Glimpse into What Comes Next

Until now, this book has examined the warning signs of wealth inequality, the historical precedents of economic injustice, and the mechanisms by which modern societies inch closer to collapse. We have explored how deregulation, political corruption, and corporate greed have exacerbated disparities, creating a fragile system where discontent festers beneath the surface. The question we must now confront is not whether this path leads to unrest—but how that unrest might unfold when the tipping point is finally reached.

History provides countless examples of economic oppression culminating in upheaval, yet no two revolutions are the same. The conditions that lead to revolt—whether gradual or explosive—are shaped by the unique circumstances of their time. In today's world, where technology accelerates communication, financial markets dictate policy, and democracy struggles to contain corporate power, the nature of revolution itself is evolving. Mass mobilization can be orchestrated with a viral tweet, financial institutions can be crippled by a few lines of malicious code, and political leaders can be held hostage—not by armies, but by public sentiment that turns against them in an instant.

To understand how the unraveling might take shape in our present era, the following narratives depict two fictional yet entirely plausible scenarios: the assassination of Jeremy Whitfield, a billionaire healthcare CEO, and the full-scale uprising that follows as the pitchforks finally arrive.

In the first, we examine a singular act of desperation that ignites a firestorm. A disenfranchised worker, drowning in medical debt, makes the fateful decision to take justice into his own hands. The assassination of Jeremy Whitfield is not just an attack on one man— it is an explosion of rage against an entire system that allowed corporate greed to override human life. It forces society to confront an uncomfortable reality: when legal avenues for change are obstructed, when suffering is monetized, and when justice is reserved only for those who can afford it, violence becomes an inevitable language of the unheard.

But the killing of one executive is merely a spark. What happens when an entire system collapses under the weight of its own failures? The second narrative envisions a world where discontent is no longer contained—where workers, activists, and the disenfranchised refuse to participate in a rigged game. Protests spiral into riots. Banks are overrun. The rich flee to their fortified enclaves, only to discover that no amount of security can protect them from a society that has decided it will no longer tolerate their excesses. The pillars of capitalism—finance, property, and corporate control—are set aflame, along with the myth that unchecked wealth accumulation can persist forever without consequence.

These fictional accounts are not predictions but warnings. They show us the breaking point—the moment when the cracks in the system can no longer be ignored. They remind us that revolutions, once ignited, rarely follow a script—and that those who believe they can control the tides of history often find themselves swept away by them.

The pitchforks are not yet in the streets, but in these next pages, we imagine what it might look like if they were.

A Healthcare CEO's Assassination: Societies Breaking Point

Narrative One: Corporate Accountability vs. Personal Tragedy
Setting the Scene: A Fictional Case Study

Imagine a not-too-distant future in which public frustration with spiraling healthcare costs, pharmaceutical price gouging, and insurance denials has reached a fever pitch. Protests erupt outside major hospitals and the headquarters of pharmaceutical giants, spurred on by viral news stories of patients dying from treatable conditions because they could not afford medication. In this climate of intensifying outrage, a high-profile healthcare CEO, whom we will call Jeremy Whitfield, is gunned down in a public parking lot.

Whitfield's role as the head of a multinational healthcare conglomerate had already drawn ire. Under his watch, the company repeatedly raised the prices of life-saving drugs, stoking controversy and condemnation from patient advocacy groups. Internal emails, leaked by a whistleblower, revealed how executives discussed profit margins in stark terms, disregarding how cost increases would devastate families dealing with chronic illnesses. These revelations prompted furious calls for Whitfield's resignation or arrest, with online commentators labeling him a "murderer in a suit." Yet no legal action ever materialized, fueling a sense that the system was rigged to protect corporate elites.

Then came the assassination. For days, #JusticeForPatients trended on social media, overshadowed only by the shock of a homicide that targeted a high-profile figure. Instantly, two conflicting narratives emerged, each catalyzed by the deep fault lines of wealth inequity.

Corporate Accountability: Symbolic Victory or Dangerous Precedent?

To some segments of the public, Whitfield's murder symbolized a form of vigilante justice. These individuals argue that after years of unchecked corporate power, which resulted in the loss of life for thousands of uninsured or underinsured patients, the system's failure to hold executives accountable inevitably led to this act of violence. They see Whitfield not as an individual victim, but as a stand-in for a corrupt healthcare industry that prioritized profit over human well-being. In their eyes, his death is less a personal tragedy and more a clarion call— a final "enough is enough" from a public at its breaking point.

This perspective echoes historical instances in which figures of concentrated power—whether feudal lords or colonial officers— were seen as fair targets by those who viewed official channels as ineffective. The moral rationale, albeit contested, posits that when systemic injustice has no viable remedies through legislation or the courts, extrajudicial measures become a last resort. Proponents of this narrative might invoke the memory of revolutions, where retribution against oppressive elites sometimes preceded more comprehensive societal change. They question whether the fear instilled by such a brazen act might force other executives and politicians to reconsider exploitative practices.

Critics, however, warn that this rationale is inherently flawed. If violence against CEOs becomes normalized, society risks descending into chaos. Vigilante acts do not guarantee constructive reforms; rather, they often provoke crackdowns, further polarizing discourse and driving moderate voices away from the public arena. Businesses might respond by increasing security measures, insulating executives more thoroughly, and refusing to engage with public demands—a stance that leads to yet more distrust rather than the resolution of systemic problems. Furthermore, the notion of "corporate accountability via assassination" sets a dangerous precedent, entrenching the idea that direct violence is the only viable recourse for those who feel aggrieved.

Personal Tragedy: The CEO as an Individual with Complex Motivations

On the other side of the ideological divide, many see Jeremy Whitfield's death as a horrific, indefensible crime. Regardless of one's views on corporate power, Whitfield was a husband, a father, and a human being with personal hopes and fears. The details of his life outside the boardroom reveal complexity: he funded scholarships for disadvantaged students, volunteered at a local youth center, and occasionally expressed personal dismay at how systemic imperatives forced drug price hikes that harmed vulnerable patients.

Those who adopt this viewpoint emphasize that the blame for exploitative healthcare practices is diffuse; it lies not just with one CEO but with an entire ecosystem, including shareholders, legislators, insurance firms, and consumer culture. Murder, they insist, cannot be condoned—even if the target is a wealthy executive deemed culpable in public opinion.

This narrative resonates with the broader principle of the rule of law, which suggests that justice should be sought through courts, regulatory bodies, and legislatures rather than individual vigilantism. By focusing on Whitfield's humanity, his family's grief, and the sudden, violent manner of his death, advocates of this interpretation seek to remind the public that moral lines should not be blurred by intense anger at systemic inequities. They warn that normalizing such acts of retribution undermines the very humanitarian values that social justice movements claim to protect.

Within this framing, the killing of Whitfield is a chilling sign of social breakdown. It reflects a moment where ordinary moral imperatives—do not kill, do not commit violence—are overshadowed by a wave of fury at corporate injustice. Those lamenting Whitfield's death believe that rather than serving as a rallying cry for systemic change, the assassination might derail serious policy discussions, enabling politicians and corporate lobbyists to paint all reformers as extremists.

Narrative Two: The Pitchforks Arrive—A Fictional Scenario of Collapse in the U.S.

It begins with a single spark—an economic shock that sends the already fragile system into chaos. A global debt crisis, triggered by financial deregulation and speculative market bubbles, causes Wall Street to implode. The stock market plunges 40% in a matter of weeks, wiping out pensions, investments, and what little savings remained for the middle class. Unemployment skyrockets as major corporations declare bankruptcy or offshore their operations to cheaper, more politically stable nations.

At the same time, inflation surges to record highs. The price of basic necessities—food, fuel, and housing—becomes unaffordable for millions of Americans. The working poor, already struggling under decades of wage stagnation, are unable to cope. Meanwhile, billionaires and multinational corporations continue to reap record profits, their wealth further shielded by offshore accounts, tax loopholes, and political influence.

In Washington, the government is paralyzed. Partisan gridlock prevents any meaningful relief package. The President—widely seen as a puppet of corporate oligarchs—offers hollow reassurances, while Congress, heavily lobbied by billionaires, refuses to pass wealth redistribution measures. State and local governments, facing insolvency, slash funding for public services, leading to widespread school closures, hospital shortages, and mass layoffs of police and emergency personnel.

The Breaking Point: The First Riots

What begins as isolated protests quickly escalates into something far more dangerous. In Chicago, a peaceful march demanding economic justice turns violent after militarized police forces clash with demonstrators. The footage of officers firing rubber bullets and tear gas into crowds of desperate, starving citizens goes viral. Across the country, frustration turns into rage.

In New York, thousands storm Wall Street. The financial district, once seen as the untouchable heart of American capitalism, is overrun by demonstrators armed with makeshift weapons— hammers, clubs, and Molotov cocktails. They break into the offices of hedge funds, smashing computers and setting fire to records. Some bankers are dragged into the streets, forced to answer for their obscene bonuses and lobbying efforts that secured their bailouts while everyday Americans lost everything. The police, overwhelmed and exhausted from days of unrest, begin to abandon their posts.

Looting spreads from city centers to suburban malls as once-law-abiding citizens realize there is no longer a functioning system of control. Armed militias, long emboldened by the country's obsession with Second Amendment rights, take matters into their own hands. Some form makeshift security forces, claiming to "restore order." Others seize the moment for political rebellion, attacking government buildings and police precincts.

In Los Angeles, the National Guard is deployed to quell riots, but soldiers—many of whom come from working-class backgrounds—begin to defect. Some openly refuse to fire on protesters, while others abandon their posts to join the rebellion. The government declares martial law, but enforcement proves impossible. Major highways are blocked, supply chains collapse, and cities plunge into darkness as power grids fail due to lack of maintenance and sabotage.

Rural America Joins the Revolt

Initially, the unrest is concentrated in urban centers, but as food shortages worsen and banks collapse, rural America follows suit. Farmers, already burdened by unsustainable debt and corporate monopolies, refuse to sell their produce to government-backed distributors. Instead, they begin trading food directly with local communities, bypassing the dollar in favor of barter economies. Independent militias seize control of key infrastructure, sabotaging oil refineries and railroads to cut off supply chains to the wealthiest enclaves.

In Texas and Florida, governors openly defy federal mandates, calling for secessionist movements. A second Civil War does not erupt overnight, but the fractures become undeniable. National unity collapses as states begin operating autonomously, rejecting federal authority and forming new alliances based on economic survival rather than party loyalty.

The Collapse of Corporate Power

For years, the wealthiest Americans believed they could shield themselves from the collapse. Gated communities, private security forces, and offshore assets had convinced them they were immune. They were wrong.

As the unrest intensifies, private security firms begin switching sides—why protect billionaires who hoard wealth while their own families starve? The ultra-rich attempt to flee via private jets, but many find the airports blockaded by desperate citizens. Those who do escape discover that their offshore havens in the Caribbean or Europe no longer welcome them. Governments abroad, fearful of their own uprisings, begin freezing American billionaires' assets and denying them entry.

Meanwhile, tech moguls who had once envisioned themselves as untouchable watch as their servers are seized, their wealth vanishes in cyber-attacks, and their influence dissolves. A group of activists infiltrates major social media networks, wiping out financial records, erasing debts, and redistributing millions in cryptocurrency to working-class citizens. The Federal Reserve is powerless to respond.

The New Order: Rebuilding Society

After months of violent upheaval, the old order collapses completely. With federal agencies effectively non-existent, new political structures emerge. In some areas, radical local governments take control, implementing wealth caps and redistributing abandoned corporate properties to the homeless and displaced. In others, worker cooperatives replace traditional businesses, forming self-sustaining economic zones.

The dollar, once the backbone of global finance, loses all value. Barter systems and digital currencies become the dominant means of exchange. Major cities, once symbols of wealth and power, are now hubs of radical change, governed by new democratic councils rather than corporate-backed politicians.

Some areas remain unstable—militias continue to fight for control, and old power structures attempt to reassert themselves. But the reality is undeniable: the America of unchecked capitalism is gone. The pitchforks came, and they did not leave until the foundations of inequality had been dismantled.

Lessons from the Fall

Historians, looking back, will not see this as an unpredictable event. The warning signs had been visible for decades—wealth inequality at historic highs, the collapse of trust in institutions, the rise of populist demagogues, and the erosion of the middle class. The elite believed they could extract wealth endlessly without consequence. They were wrong.

Revolutions are rarely planned. They are sparked by desperation, fueled by anger, and driven by the simple reality that people, when pushed too far, will push back.

The pitchforks did not come in the way the elite imagined—not as isolated riots, but as a systemic collapse of the very structures they had relied upon to maintain power. And as history has shown time and again, when the people rise, the old order falls.

The Breaking Point: When Inequality Sparks Revolution

The warning signs had been there for decades—rising wealth inequality, stagnant wages, corporate greed, and political corruption. Yet those in power ignored them, convinced that they could continue extracting wealth from the working class without consequence. But history has never been kind to elites who mistake silence for compliance. Eventually, people rise.

In a country where billionaires built empires on the backs of underpaid labor while ordinary families struggled to afford healthcare and housing, the tension had reached a boiling point.

When the first act of violence came, many dismissed it as an isolated event. They were wrong. It was simply the first of the dominoes to fall.

The Assassination That Sparked the Revolt

It started with a single, shocking act. A high-profile CEO of a major healthcare conglomerate was assassinated while delivering a keynote speech in Washington, D.C. The shooter, later identified as a former nurse burdened by medical debt and unable to afford his wife's cancer treatment, had left behind a manifesto. In it, he blamed the healthcare industry for prioritizing profits over human lives. The video of the incident spread like wildfire, igniting widespread protests and mass unrest.

Initially, the government treated the assassination as an isolated incident—a tragic, senseless crime. But for millions of Americans drowning in medical debt, unable to afford basic necessities, and watching their wages stagnate while executive bonuses soared, it was anything but senseless. It was a message.

As crowds gathered outside hospitals and pharmaceutical headquarters, chanting for justice, law enforcement cracked down violently. Riot police deployed tear gas and rubber bullets, arresting hundreds. But instead of quelling the unrest, the crackdown only fueled the fire. The protests spread across the country.

Labor unions, long suppressed by corporate interests, saw an opportunity and called for nationwide strikes. Public transit shut down in major cities. Truckers refused to deliver goods. Supermarket shelves emptied within days.

In desperation, the government declared a state of emergency, but it was too late. The economy was grinding to a halt, and people were beginning to realize their collective power.

The Arrival of the Pitchforks

For weeks, the country teetered on the edge of collapse. The rich continued to retreat behind their gated communities, guarded by private security firms. But then, the system itself buckled. Banks, already struggling with economic instability, froze withdrawals. The stock market crashed. Unemployment skyrocketed as businesses shut down en masse. The illusion of stability crumbled, and the fragile trust holding society together shattered. The people had nothing left to lose.

The first large-scale riot took place in New York City. Thousands of protesters stormed Wall Street, setting fire to hedge fund offices and ransacking corporate headquarters. When the National Guard was deployed, many of the soldiers refused to fire on the protesters—many of them had families suffering from the same financial hardships. Entire battalions defected, leaving the government's ability to enforce control in doubt.

The uprising spread across the country. In Los Angeles, protesters took over wealthy neighborhoods, looting mansions and redistributing food and supplies. Tech billionaires found their estates surrounded by angry mobs demanding justice for decades of economic exploitation. Some attempted to flee the country, but airports were blocked, and foreign governments, wary of the instability, refused them entry.

In Washington, the government was in full crisis mode. Martial law was declared, but with police forces overwhelmed and military defections increasing, enforcement was nearly impossible. As the government collapsed under the weight of its own failures, local communities began forming their own governance structures. Neighborhood councils took over essential services. Barter economies emerged as the dollar lost value. In some areas, worker cooperatives replaced traditional businesses, redistributing abandoned corporate assets to former employees.

Analysis: The Seeds of Collapse

Both the assassination of the healthcare CEO and the full-scale uprising that followed were not spontaneous events. They were the result of years—decades—of systemic injustice. Societies do not collapse overnight. Revolutions are not random; they are built on long-standing grievances, eroded trust, and a sense of collective betrayal.

The assassination was symbolic. It was the moment when the oppressed struck back in a way that could no longer be ignored. It was not just about one man or one industry—it was about an entire system that had devalued human life in the pursuit of profits. It exposed the raw desperation of a population pushed beyond its limits. The government's response—violent suppression—was the catalyst that transformed a single act of violence into a national movement.

The full-scale revolt that followed was predictable. The signs had been there: declining wages, rising inflation, political corruption, and corporate greed. The failure of democratic institutions to address these problems meant that people turned to more extreme measures. Historically, every major revolution has followed this same pattern: the people demand change, the government resists, and when repression reaches its peak, the system collapses.

The fatal mistake of the elite was believing that their wealth and power made them untouchable. They built security forces, lobbied for laws that protected them from accountability, and hoarded resources while the rest of the country starved. But when the very foundations of society—banks, food distribution, law enforcement—collapsed, their power crumbled. Their wealth, once a fortress, became a target.

The Lessons We Ignore at Our Own Peril

The scenario described here is, of course, fictional, but it is not far-fetched. The warning signs of societal collapse are visible today—growing economic disparity, a political system that serves the few over the many, and a population growing increasingly restless.

History has shown us what happens when inequality reaches unsustainable levels. The French Revolution, the Russian Revolution, and, more recently, the Arab Spring all began with economic injustices pushing ordinary people past their breaking points. Each time, the elite underestimated the anger of the masses. Each time, they believed the status quo could hold indefinitely. And each time, they were wrong.

The difference between history and our present moment is that we still have time. The pitchforks are not yet in the streets—but they are being sharpened. The anger is real, the desperation is growing, and the social fabric is fraying. There are two paths forward. One leads to reform—an acknowledgment that extreme inequality is unsustainable and that systemic change is necessary. The other leads to collapse, where the people, left with no other options, take matters into their own hands.

If we ignore these warning signs, we will not be able to claim ignorance when the pitchforks finally arrive.

Conclusion: Charting the Aftermath

In these chapters, I have sought to illustrate how modern societies, particularly those in the West, stand at a crossroads. If wealth inequality continues unabated, the consequences will not be abstract—they will be real, immediate, and potentially irreversible. The revolutions of the past may have been marked by barricades and guillotines, but in the digital era, mass mobilization takes new forms. Social media, encrypted networks, and decentralized movements have replaced backroom conspiracies and clandestine meetings. Yet, despite these new tools, the fundamental drivers of revolt remain unchanged—anger, betrayal, and the desperate need for justice.

The assassination of a healthcare CEO, while fictional, serves as a stark warning of how far disillusionment can drive those who feel abandoned by the system. It is easy to dismiss such an act as the work of a lone extremist, but it would be a mistake to ignore the deeper rot that makes such violence conceivable. When official channels fail to deliver justice, when lawmakers prioritize corporate donors over struggling citizens, when the wealthiest exploit suffering to maximize profit—rage does not simply disappear. It festers. It waits. And then, when the right spark is struck, it erupts.

Yet the question remains: What does justice look like in a world where the pitchforks can take many forms—hashtags, bullets, mass boycotts, or mobs storming financial districts? It is a question without easy answers. Revolution can be a force for progress, reshaping societies in ways that expand democracy, safeguard rights, and rebalance power. But history is also filled with revolutions that devoured themselves—movements that began in the name of justice but ended in paranoia, purges, and authoritarianism. The forces that ignite revolution are not always the same ones that guide its aftermath.

Technology accelerates this paradox. In one moment, it is a tool of liberation—amplifying voices, exposing injustices, and connecting the disaffected. In the next, it becomes a weapon of surveillance and control, turning those same voices into targets for suppression. The same algorithm that enables grassroots movements can also be used to dismantle them. The same networks that spread truth can also be weaponized to sow division. In this volatile landscape, the line between resistance and retribution blurs.

What this book argues, and what Part III will expand upon, is that the greatest danger is not in the inevitability of revolution, but in the refusal to acknowledge its causes. History is filled with examples of societies ignoring the warning signs of collapse— mistaking momentary calm for lasting stability. The data points are always there before the storm: widening economic divides, collapsing trust in institutions, declining social mobility. The wealthy, convinced of their invincibility, retreat into fortified compounds, building walls rather than bridges. The poor, denied opportunity, watch as their futures slip further out of reach.

And then, one day, the dam breaks.

But history also offers an alternative path—one where the powerful recognize the need for change before it is too late. There have been moments when societies have pulled back from the abyss, implementing bold reforms that recalibrated economic structures and restored faith in governance. Franklin Roosevelt's New Deal, for example, prevented the U.S. from sliding into full-scale revolt during the Great Depression. Scandinavian social democracies successfully blended capitalism with robust welfare systems, proving that equitable economies need not be utopian fantasies. The question now is whether today's leaders—political, corporate, and civic—will heed these lessons.

If they do, the need for pitchforks can be defused. If they don't, the arrival of unrest becomes a matter of when, not if.

As the next part of this book will explore, solutions exist. But they require more than token gestures or rhetorical flourishes. We must rethink how wealth is created, who benefits from it, and what role economic justice plays in sustaining democracy itself. This means addressing taxation, regulation, labor protections, and the unchecked power of corporations in shaping public policy. It means recognizing that inequality is not a symptom of capitalism gone awry—it is a direct consequence of how modern capitalism has been structured.

The story of Jeremy Whitfield, fictional though it may be, forces us to confront the moral, political, and economic dilemmas at the heart of this debate. His actions—whether seen as terrorism or righteous retribution—are less about one man's choices and more about a system that allowed his anger to fester. The true question we must ask is not whether people will lash out at injustice, but whether we will create a world where they no longer feel the need to.

For better or worse, the specter of revolution looms over the 21st century. It will be shaped by technology, by ideology, and by the increasingly desperate calls for economic justice. The key to preventing collapse lies in acknowledging that wealth inequality is not a temporary crisis—it is the defining fault line of our time. Addressing it requires structural change, not band-aid solutions. Whether that change is embraced peacefully or forced upon the powerful through upheaval remains the central dilemma of the modern age.

Part IV
Rebalancing Society

Introduction

As I have tried to show throughout this book, wealth inequity is not merely an economic statistic; rather, it is a condition that underpins social unrest, political upheaval, and a fragile civic order. The earlier sections explored how disparities in income and resources can fuel discontent, fracture political systems, and heighten the risk of collective turmoil—even in societies that pride themselves on strong democratic norms. The trajectory we have traced so far—from warnings by the wealthy themselves and the seeds of global resentment to political disruptions and visions of modern insurrection—underscores a critical need for fundamental change.

In writing *Part IV: Rebalancing Society*, I aim to focus on potential solutions and frameworks for creating a more equitable world. These are not utopian fantasies or abstract economic theories. Rather, I believe they represent practical strategies—many of which have been tested in various contexts—that can help stabilize and renew the social contract binding governments, businesses, and citizens. Across four chapters in this section, I will examine corporate responsibility, governance reforms, the construction of a new social contract, and, finally, a call to action that envisions a cohesive partnership among the key actors in our societies.

As a reader, you may ask: Is it truly possible to achieve a fairer distribution of wealth without undermining the incentives that drive innovation and prosperity? Can companies and governments realistically act in tandem to ensure workers are paid living wages, essential services remain accessible, and democratic processes stay robust—without crushing free enterprise? It is easy to be skeptical, particularly given the entrenched interests and complexities of modern capitalism. Yet history shows that meaningful progress often arises from moments of crisis or when glaring moral imperatives become impossible to ignore. If anything, the sobering realities of mounting unrest and systemic fragility should galvanize us to explore new paradigms.

At this critical juncture, we have a choice: We can cling to existing structures, hoping for incremental improvements, or we can muster the political and ethical will for transformative change. *Rebalancing Society* outlines a path for the latter, providing a framework that empowers workers, holds corporations accountable, and refashions governance in ways that promote shared prosperity. As you read the chapters that follow, remember that the future is neither preordained nor static. The decisions we make today will determine whether we avert the worst-case scenarios depicted earlier in this book— forging instead a fairer, more resilient global community.

The Corporate Responsibility Revolution

The Moral and Financial Case for Fair Wages

One of the most pressing concerns highlighted by recent social movements is the persistent gap between corporate profits and worker compensation. The moral argument for paying workers a fair wage is compelling on its face: When people labor full-time (or even part-time) for a company, they deserve to earn enough to cover basic living costs such as shelter, nourishment, healthcare, and education. This concept forms the bedrock of *social citizenship* in any advanced society, implying that economic participants should be protected from destitution and exploitation.

Yet the case for fair wages goes beyond morality. There is also a sound financial logic that benefits companies, economies, and societies at large. Corporations rely on consumer spending to generate revenue. If workers—who often make up the bulk of any consumer base—cannot afford to purchase products and services, then overall economic growth stagnates. By contrast, raising wages can stimulate a virtuous cycle: With greater disposable income, workers purchase more goods, encouraging firms to invest further in production, thereby creating new jobs. This phenomenon was observed in the post-World War II era when rising wages and increased consumer demand fueled decades of economic expansion in the United States and several European nations.

Productivity and Employee Engagement

A key dimension of the fair wage discussion is productivity. Many firms mistakenly assume that suppressing labor costs is the optimal path to higher profits. However, empirical research reveals a more nuanced picture. Employees who feel valued—reflected in adequate compensation, benefits, and a sense of ownership in the company—tend to be more motivated, creative, and loyal. Their increased engagement can lead to higher-quality work, better customer service, and lower turnover rates. By contrast, companies that pay the bare minimum often face high staff attrition, weak morale, and reputational harm.

From a pragmatic standpoint, offering fair wages can reduce recruitment and training costs over the long run. High turnover imposes hidden but significant expenses, including advertising job vacancies, interviewing candidates, and onboarding new hires. When viewed through this lens, pay equity emerges as an investment in a firm's human capital rather than a simple outlay.

Wages as a Tool to Combat Inequality

Beyond the corporate perimeter, fair wages serve as a cornerstone of any strategy to combat broader wealth inequity. If companies adopt a standard of paying *living wages* rather than *minimum wages*, a large section of society will be lifted to more comfortable economic ground, reducing reliance on government assistance programs and lowering the incidence of poverty-related social ills—such as poor health outcomes and elevated crime rates.

A well-designed wage system can also mitigate the gender pay gap, racial disparities in income, and intergenerational poverty. In such an environment, families are better able to invest in the education and health of their children, sowing the seeds for a more prosperous future for all.

Still, skeptics worry that raising wages too rapidly might undermine competitiveness, particularly in labor-intensive industries. However, examples from countries like Germany and certain states in the United States—where wage floors have been incrementally increased—show that adverse impacts can be mitigated if implemented gradually and paired with supportive policies such as tax credits or subsidized training. The key is to view fair wages as part of a broader ecosystem of corporate social responsibility rather than as an isolated legislative imposition.

Redistributing Wealth Without Destroying Capitalism

The term "redistribution" often evokes fears of heavy-handed government intervention and the erosion of free-market dynamics. Critics question whether capitalism can remain innovative and competitive if wealth is reallocated from the upper tiers of society to those lower on the economic ladder. However, history and contemporary economic theory suggest that capitalism can indeed survive—and even thrive—under balanced redistributive mechanisms. The essential task is to ensure that such mechanisms do not stifle entrepreneurial spirit or unfairly penalize success.

Shareholder vs. Stakeholder Capitalism

One of the foundational shifts in modern corporate responsibility lies in moving beyond a narrow shareholder-centric model. Traditional capitalism often tasks CEOs and boards with a fiduciary duty to maximize shareholder returns, sometimes at the expense of employees, consumers, and local communities. By contrast, a stakeholder model of capitalism broadens the scope of corporate accountability. Companies are encouraged—or even legally mandated—to factor in the interests of workers, local residents, environmental concerns, and future generations.

Practical strategies include integrating sustainability metrics into performance evaluations, offering workers avenues for collective decision-making, and forging closer relationships with local suppliers. These approaches do not necessarily diminish profits; rather, they foster a more sustainable and holistic form of value creation, shielding companies from reputational damage, consumer boycotts, and the long-term costs of environmental degradation.

Incentivizing Fairness: Bonus Caps and Progressive Executive Pay

Executive pay has long been a flashpoint in debates about wealth inequity. Cases of CEOs earning hundreds of times more than their average employees—while workers struggle to afford rent or basic healthcare—fuel public indignation. Yet capping executive pay outright can be politically unpalatable and may deter top talent.

Instead, policies that tie executive bonuses to factors beyond short-term share price—such as employee satisfaction, environmental performance, and community engagement—can align the interests of top management with broader societal goals.

Some companies have experimented with capping pay multiples, ensuring the highest-paid executive does not earn more than a certain ratio relative to the median employee salary. Others have adopted profit-sharing schemes, distributing a fixed percentage of the firm's annual earnings among all staff. These measures reframe compensation as a collective endeavor: success is rewarded across the organization rather than pooling disproportionately at the top. Although such policies require delicate calibration to avoid undue bureaucratic complexity, they send a strong signal that the firm values equity and long-term stability over short-term gains.

Encouraging Social Enterprise and B-Corps

Another avenue to redistribute wealth without dismantling capitalist principles is through the promotion of social enterprises and Benefit Corporations (B-Corps). These entities commit to social or environmental missions alongside profit objectives, embedding more equitable outcomes into their core business practices. They are legally bound to consider stakeholder interests, ensuring that the pursuit of profit does not overshadow the public good.

While it's not a panacea for systemic inequality, the growth of the B-Corp movement indicates a desire among entrepreneurs, consumers, and investors for a new business paradigm—one in which wealth generation is accompanied by social responsibility. Governments can encourage such initiatives through tax incentives, preferential public procurement policies, or supportive legal frameworks. Over time, the mainstreaming of social enterprise could reshape public perception of what "successful" business looks like, shifting the cultural focus from unbridled profit to accountable, sustainable growth.

Reforming Governance

Progressive Taxation and Closing Loopholes

When discussing solutions to wealth inequity, one cannot ignore the pivotal role of fiscal policy. Governments that fail to collect adequate revenue from their wealthiest citizens and largest corporations invariably leave the burden of funding public services on the less well-off. Progressive taxation, which levies higher rates on those with greater means, has historically been a mainstay of strategies to reduce glaring wealth disparities.

The Rationale for Progressive Taxes

Progressive taxation ensures that as individuals and corporations climb the income ladder, they contribute proportionally more to the common good. The moral justification is straightforward: those who have gained the most from an economic system should reinvest in its upkeep and the welfare of the society from which they derived their prosperity. Economically, progressive taxes can help stabilize consumer demand. When disposable income is more evenly distributed, it can bolster market vitality, especially in consumer-driven economies.

Contrary to alarmist claims, progressive taxation does not automatically drive away capital or deter investment. While there are indeed thresholds beyond which high earners might choose to relocate, evidence from Nordic countries suggests that well-structured tax regimes—coupled with quality public services—can actually enhance economic competitiveness. Quality healthcare, education, and infrastructure, funded through robust taxation, can be attractive to businesses seeking healthy, educated workforces and well-maintained environments.

Closing Loopholes and Offshoring Schemes

A pressing issue in modern fiscal policy is the use of tax havens, shell companies, and other legal structures that enable corporations and wealthy individuals to avoid paying their fair share. The *Panama Papers* and similar leaks have revealed how deeply entrenched these practices are, siphoning trillions of dollars out of national coffers. Despite token efforts to crack down on offshoring, many loopholes remain intact.

Reforming governance to address tax avoidance requires both international coordination and domestic resolve. Bilateral or multilateral treaties can disincentivize profit-shifting, requiring companies to pay taxes in the jurisdictions where their income is actually generated. Transparent accounting standards and public registries of beneficial ownership can also make it harder to hide assets behind complex networks of subsidiaries. Ultimately, the goal is to eliminate the perverse incentives that reward moving wealth to secrecy jurisdictions, thereby restoring equity and fairness in how taxes are collected.

Smart Redistribution: Public Investments in the Common Good

Revenue raised through progressive taxation and loophole closures should be directed toward programs that foster social mobility and community resilience. This includes funding universal healthcare, robust public education, affordable housing schemes, and grants for small enterprises. By channeling funds into projects that have broad societal benefits, governments can mitigate criticism that taxation is merely punitive. Instead, taxes become a tool for catalyzing opportunity and security, helping to build a more inclusive economy in which fewer people feel compelled to mount the proverbial "pitchforks."

Empowering Unions and Worker Representation

Democratic governance extends beyond the confines of parliamentary politics; it also includes the economic sphere, where workers' voices have historically been channeled through labor unions. However, union membership has declined sharply in many Western nations over the past few decades, in part due to hostile legislation, corporate resistance, and structural changes in employment (such as the rise of gig work).

The Relevance of Unions in the Modern Economy

Unions have long been at the forefront of campaigns for better wages, safer working conditions, and more equitable profit-sharing. In periods of growing inequality, strong unions can act as a countervailing force against unchecked corporate power. They provide a platform for collective bargaining, ensuring that workers do not have to negotiate employment terms in isolation. Beyond this, unions often serve as community anchors, offering legal advice, skills training, and a cohesive social network for members.

Critics argue that unions can become complacent or overly adversarial, hindering productivity. While there is a kernel of truth in some criticisms—particularly where union leadership becomes entangled in bureaucratic politics—robust unions, when responsibly managed, can actively contribute to workplace innovation. They facilitate dialogue between management and labor, enabling both sides to address inefficiencies, propose new work patterns, or adopt technological solutions that enhance productivity without imposing disproportionate burdens on workers.

Legislative Support for Collective Bargaining

To revitalize union power, governments might enact legislation that protects the right to organize, prohibits anti-union tactics such as firing activists, and promotes sector-wide bargaining frameworks. In some European countries, collective agreements are negotiated at an industry level, setting baseline wages and conditions across multiple firms. This "social partnership" model reduces the chances that companies will undercut each other on labor costs, making the entire economic ecosystem more equitable.

An effective legislative environment also addresses the unique challenges posed by the gig economy, where workers are often classified as independent contractors with limited bargaining rights. Clear standards that define "employment" and "benefits eligibility" can close loopholes, preventing companies from exploiting precarious labor. The potential benefits of such reforms are immense: by instilling a sense of dignity and agency among workers, societies can reduce income disparities and quell the anger that fuels populist and extremist movements.

Worker Representation on Corporate Boards

A more transformative approach involves mandating worker representation on corporate boards, a practice already in place in certain countries. In Germany, for instance, large firms are required by law to allocate up to half of board seats to employee representatives. This model, known as "co-determination," ensures that decisions about corporate strategy, mergers, layoffs, and investment plans cannot be made without input from those whose livelihoods depend on the enterprise.

Co-determination has been credited with maintaining industrial peace and forging collaborative relationships between management and unions. While no system is without flaws, the German experience reveals that worker representation can encourage long-term thinking, sustain higher wages, and foster an atmosphere of mutual respect. Critics argue that such policies could hamper competitiveness, yet Germany's globally recognized manufacturing prowess challenges that assumption, indicating that worker empowerment and economic success need not be mutually exclusive.

Building a New Social Contract

Universal Basic Income and Affordable Housing

Central to rebalancing society is the notion of a new social contract—one that comprehensively addresses the essential needs of citizens. Two policy proposals have gained considerable traction in this regard: Universal Basic Income (UBI) and expanded affordable housing initiatives. Both measures aim to provide a baseline of security, mitigating the precariousness that arises from market-based living costs and erratic employment opportunities.

Universal Basic Income: A Safety Net for the 21st Century

UBI typically entails regular cash payments from the government to all individuals or households, regardless of income or employment status. Proponents see UBI as a hedge against job displacement driven by automation and globalized competition, offering financial stability to people whose industries might vanish or whose skills become obsolete. With a guaranteed income floor, recipients can afford to take entrepreneurial risks, invest in further education, or reduce overwork, potentially leading to more dynamic labor markets and healthier, more engaged communities.

Opponents question the affordability of UBI, worrying that it could exacerbate inflation or disincentivize the search for gainful employment. However, pilot programs in places like Finland and parts of Canada have not shown large-scale declines in workforce participation. The cost of UBI is also offset by reductions in administrative overhead for multiple means-tested welfare programs and by the societal benefits of less poverty-induced crime and reduced healthcare expenditures. If carefully designed, funded, and incrementally introduced, UBI could stabilize communities, alleviate the fear of destitution, and narrow the gap between rich and poor.

Affordable Housing as an Economic and Social Priority

Housing ranks among the largest expenses for the average household, and in major urban centers, rising property prices and rents can drive low- and middle-income residents out of their neighborhoods. Lack of access to safe, affordable housing contributes to homelessness, ill health, and entrenched social disadvantage. It also exacerbates wealth inequity, as housing assets often form a significant portion of family wealth for the middle class.

Addressing the housing crisis calls for a multi-pronged approach. Governments can invest in social housing, offering below-market rents to those in need. Policies like rent control, though contentious, can shield tenants from sudden spikes in property values. At the same time, initiatives that incentivize the construction of mid-range housing can expand the supply of homes that the average worker can afford. Zoning reforms are another crucial element, ensuring that cities do not become exclusive enclaves reserved for the affluent. Streamlined planning processes, combined with public subsidies for low-income units, can balance development interests with the public's right to decent living conditions.

A robust housing policy has ripple effects. If people are not constantly struggling to cover extortionate rent, they have more disposable income to circulate in local economies, more time and emotional energy to participate in civic life, and a stable home base for children's education. Placing housing security at the heart of a new social contract acknowledges that the ability to thrive—economically and socially—depends on having a roof over one's head.

Ensuring Equal Access to Education and Healthcare

A well-functioning society depends on an educated, healthy populace. In many Western nations, the rising costs of higher education, coupled with healthcare expenses, perpetuate cycles of disadvantage. The new social contract thus includes commitments to accessible education and healthcare for all, recognizing these as foundational to both individual dignity and collective prosperity.

Equitable Education: From Early Childhood to University Level

Educational inequities often begin early. Children from low-income families may lack access to high-quality early childhood programs, putting them at a disadvantage even before starting primary school. Underfunded public schools compound these challenges, leading to achievement gaps that persist well into adolescence and adulthood. By contrast, wealthy families can invest in private schooling, extracurricular activities, and educational technologies, amplifying their advantage.

Addressing these disparities involves more than just increasing budgets. It requires a holistic strategy: smaller class sizes, well-trained teachers, nutritious school meals, and robust student support services. Technology can play a democratizing role if it is accessible to all, bridging learning gaps rather than widening them. At the tertiary level, reducing tuition costs—or eliminating them altogether—helps ensure that university is not a privilege reserved for the children of affluent families. Grant programs, income-based repayment plans, and robust scholarships can lessen the burden of student debt, allowing graduates to pursue careers aligned with their skills and passions rather than feeling compelled to chase the highest-paying job simply to manage loan repayments.

Universal Healthcare: A Moral and Economic Imperative

Healthcare systems across the world vary dramatically, but a common thread in countries with high levels of inequality is that the

101

best care often goes to those with the most resources. Even in nations with nominally universal healthcare, gaps in coverage, long waiting times, or out-of-pocket expenses can create de facto tiers of service.

The moral argument for universal healthcare is straightforward: no person should be denied medical treatment due to an inability to pay. Economically, preventing serious illnesses or chronic conditions through accessible preventive care can save enormous sums in the long run.

Models range from fully state-funded systems, like the National Health Service in the United Kingdom, to multi-payer systems with tight regulation, such as in Germany or the Netherlands. While each approach has pros and cons, the overarching principle remains that healthcare should not be a commodified good, subject to the profit motives of private insurers or pharmaceutical companies at the expense of public well-being. By redirecting resources toward preventive measures, mental health support, and equitable access to treatments, societies can not only improve quality of life but also enhance economic productivity, as healthier populations are more energetic and capable of contributing to civic and economic endeavors.

The Path Forward: A Call to Action

Collaboration Between Governments, Businesses, and Citizens

Successfully rebalancing society is a complex task. It demands concerted efforts from multiple stakeholders who may not always see eye to eye. Governments must bring legislative and regulatory power, setting the framework that holds corporations accountable and ensures that the fruits of growth are shared more broadly. Businesses, particularly large corporations, wield enormous economic clout and possess the capacity to shape social outcomes— either by embracing corporate responsibility or resisting changes that might limit short-term profits. Citizens, for their part, have the power to organize, vote, and shift cultural norms, exercising a collective influence that can realign political agendas.

Multi-Stakeholder Platforms and Policy Co-Creation

One potential avenue for meaningful cooperation is the formation of multi-stakeholder platforms, where government officials, business leaders, union representatives, and civil society groups engage in dialogue. These platforms can set shared objectives—for instance, reducing child poverty by half within a decade—and negotiate specific policies, timelines, and accountability measures. Policy co-creation shifts governance away from top-down edicts, recognizing that complex social challenges require insights from all sides.

Such initiatives already exist in various forms, such as sectoral councils in Scandinavian countries or local community boards in some American cities. The principle is the same: harness diverse perspectives to craft solutions that are both economically viable and socially progressive. While this process can be slow and prone to political squabbling, it also yields policies with broader legitimacy, reducing the likelihood of abrupt reversals when political power changes hands.

Public-Private Partnerships for Infrastructure and Services

In addition to multi-stakeholder forums, public-private partnerships (PPPs) can play a constructive role in addressing societal needs. By pooling resources and expertise, governments and businesses can expand essential infrastructure—transport, broadband internet, green energy—without placing the entire fiscal burden on taxpayers. Well-structured PPPs must include robust oversight to prevent profiteering or substandard service delivery, but when carefully managed, they can accelerate the development of physical and digital infrastructure that underpins inclusive growth.

Collaboration is also crucial in the realm of education and vocational training. With rapid technological changes reshaping job markets, governments can provide frameworks for lifelong learning programs, while businesses supply expertise, funding, and placement opportunities. This synergy ensures that training is relevant to real-world demand, equipping workers to adapt to emerging industries and reducing the labor market polarization that contributes to inequality.

A Vision for a Balanced, Just, and Prosperous Society

As we draw this part of the book to a close, it is vital to articulate a coherent vision of the society we wish to build. Rebalancing society is not about leveling everyone to the same economic plane or stifling entrepreneurial ambition. Nor is it about turning the state into an overbearing presence in everyday life. Rather, it seeks a social and economic order in which prosperity is shared, dignity is preserved, and democratic values are upheld.

Balancing Markets and Morality

At the heart of this vision is a balance between markets and morality. Markets excel at allocating resources, fostering innovation, and rewarding productivity. However, markets untempered by ethical and regulatory frameworks can devolve into engines of exploitation and environmental harm. By setting guardrails—fair wages, progressive taxes, union rights, and strong antitrust enforcement—society ensures that market forces contribute to collective well-being rather than engendering turmoil.

Moreover, the moral dimension extends beyond economics to cultural attitudes. The notion that some lives are worth more than others or that certain groups are intrinsically more deserving of privilege is incompatible with a just society. Embracing diversity, tackling discrimination, and providing universal social provisions are not "charitable" gestures; they are cornerstones of stable, prosperous nations.

Harnessing Innovation for the Common Good

In a rebalanced society, innovation—be it technological, scientific, or organizational—serves the common good. Public funding for research and development can expand to areas that yield broad societal benefits, from renewable energy to affordable medical treatments. Intellectual property laws can be recalibrated to encourage collaborative breakthroughs rather than creating artificial monopolies that restrict access to life-saving drugs or emergent climate solutions.

Importantly, harnessing innovation in a just manner involves acknowledging that automation and AI will continue to disrupt labor markets. Rather than lamenting this trend, a forward-looking approach invests in upskilling, retraining, and transitional support for displaced workers. By combining these measures with universal basic income (UBI) or robust social safety nets, societies can ensure that technological advancements do not produce a permanent underclass but rather open pathways to new forms of work and creativity.

Cultivating Ethical Leadership and Global Responsibility

Rebalancing society is not solely a domestic undertaking; it also entails recognizing and fulfilling obligations toward the global community. Nations should collaborate on climate change mitigation, poverty reduction, and international tax cooperation, acting on the understanding that problems such as environmental degradation or large-scale migration cannot be contained by national borders. Richer countries can fund development programs or share technologies with poorer nations, reducing global inequities that feed instability and mass displacement.

This sense of global responsibility is mirrored in the call for ethical leadership at every level, from local councils to multinational corporations. Leaders who value transparency, accountability, and empathy can build trust, even when faced with tough decisions. Institutions that promote such leaders and remove those who exploit power for personal gain stand a better chance of enacting lasting reforms.

Conclusion

I hope that *Part IV: Rebalancing Society* has outlined the practical steps and overarching philosophies that can guide us from a fractious, unequal present toward a more inclusive, stable future. From ensuring fair wages to strengthening unions, from progressive taxation to universal basic income and healthcare, these proposals address multiple facets of the same fundamental issue: the widening gulf between the privileged few and the struggling many. They also highlight the importance of cross-sector cooperation, moral leadership, and the recognition that market mechanisms alone cannot ensure justice.

The solutions proposed here are neither simplistic nor uniform. They demand careful calibration to local contexts, ideological openness, and sustained political will. Critics may see them as too radical or, conversely, too modest. Yet the core premise stands: if we refuse to act, the dire predictions of civil unrest and socio-political fragmentation loom ever larger. The "pitchforks," whether literal or metaphorical, are a call to urgency. Our task is to heed that call and forge pathways that preserve the best of our innovative, free-market traditions while eradicating the cruel inequities that sow discord and despair.

This does not mean eliminating wealth or success. On the contrary, a well-regulated, stakeholder-focused market can continue to generate prosperity but in a manner that is inclusive and socially responsible. Our moment in history cries out for a bold reset—a comprehensive reevaluation of how wealth is generated, distributed, and utilized in service of the common good. Achieving such a rebalancing is an arduous endeavor, but it is also the path most likely to secure a future in which the horrors of violent revolution are replaced by genuine, collective progress.

It may be tempting to see these aspirations as unrealistic in the face of entrenched power structures and cultural inertia. Yet history teaches that societies can change course when motivated by moral clarity and pragmatic self-interest. Given the threats outlined in previous parts of this book—from populist turmoil to catastrophic social breakdown—it becomes clear that doing nothing is no longer an option.

Instead, let us commit to the ongoing work of building a society worthy of its highest ideals—one where justice, dignity, and opportunity are truly shared by all.

Conclusion

The Warning and the Opportunity

Throughout this book, I have sought to illustrate the deepening crisis of wealth concentration and its potential consequences for modern society. The warning is clear: if economic disparity continues unchecked, the result will be widespread instability, social unrest, and systemic collapse. However, this trajectory is not inevitable. With proactive measures, we still have the opportunity to change course, forging a more equitable and sustainable economic system that benefits all rather than just the privileged few.

The Pitchforks Are Coming, But They Don't Have to Be

History provides countless examples of what happens when inequality spirals out of control. The collapse of monarchies, the rise of revolutions, and the fall of empires all stem from a common cause—an imbalance of wealth and power that left the majority of people disillusioned, angry, and desperate for change.

Today, the warning signs are unmistakable. Rising populism, political instability, and increasing distrust in institutions are symptoms of a deeper, more fundamental crisis. If we continue along this path, a tipping point is inevitable.

But history is not fate. Societies have, at times, recognized these warning signs and made course corrections before full-scale collapse. The choice before us is simple: either we take meaningful steps to address inequity now, or we allow economic and political fractures to deepen until they explode in ways that no government, corporation, or financial institution can control.

Rewriting the Rules of Wealth, Power, and Humanity

Reversing the tide of wealth concentration will require more than just policy adjustments—it demands a structural and cultural shift in how wealth and power are distributed. This means bold reforms: progressive taxation that ensures corporations and billionaires pay their fair share, reinvestment in social infrastructure such as healthcare, education, and housing, and a rebalancing of labor rights to ensure workers receive fair wages and protections.

It also requires a shift in priorities, from maximizing short-term profits to fostering long-term economic sustainability and social well-being.

The pitchforks may not be in the streets today, but they are dangerously close. When frustration turns to fury and systems fail to deliver fairness, people will eventually take matters into their own hands. Revolutions do not begin with sudden outbursts—they are the culmination of years of injustice, eroded trust, and economic exploitation. The warning signs are all around us, and without meaningful reform, the breaking point will come.

Yet there is still time to rewrite this story. The opportunity remains to build an economic system that values human dignity, fairness, and shared prosperity. A more just society is not only a moral imperative—it is the only sustainable path forward.

But the window for change is closing. The choice is ours: act now or wait until the pitchforks are no longer just a metaphor.

References

The following sources have been referenced or have influenced the research and perspectives presented in this book:

- Hanauer, N. (2014). *Beware, Fellow Plutocrats, the Pitchforks Are Coming*. TED Talks. [Online] Available at: https://www.ted.com/talks/nick_hanauer_beware_fellow_plutocrats_the_pitchforks_are_coming

- Piketty, T. (2014). *Capital in the Twenty-First Century*. Harvard University Press.

- Stiglitz, J. (2012). *The Price of Inequality: How Today's Divided Society Endangers Our Future*. W.W. Norton & Company.

- Milanovic, B. (2016). *Global Inequality: A New Approach for the Age of Globalization*. Harvard University Press.

- Graeber, D. (2011). *Debt: The First 5000 Years*. Melville House.

- Polanyi, K. (1944). *The Great Transformation: The Political and Economic Origins of Our Time*. Beacon Press.

- Saez, E. & Zucman, G. (2019). *The Triumph of Injustice: How the Rich Dodge Taxes and How to Make Them Pay*. W.W. Norton & Company.

- Acemoglu, D. & Robinson, J. (2012). *Why Nations Fail: The Origins of Power, Prosperity, and Poverty*. Crown Business.

- Varoufakis, Y. (2017). *Talking to My Daughter About the Economy: A Brief History of Capitalism*. Farrar, Straus and Giroux.

- Zuboff, S. (2019). *The Age of Surveillance Capitalism: The Fight for a Human Future at the New Frontier of Power*. PublicAffairs.

- Harvey, D. (2005). *A Brief History of Neoliberalism*. Oxford University Press.

- Monbiot, G. (2017). *Out of the Wreckage: A New Politics for an Age of Crisis*. Verso Books.

- Klein, N. (2007). *The Shock Doctrine: The Rise of Disaster Capitalism*. Penguin Books.

- Chomsky, N. (1999). *Profit Over People: Neoliberalism and Global Order*. Seven Stories Press.

- Pistor, K. (2019). *The Code of Capital: How the Law Creates Wealth and Inequality*. Princeton University Press.

- Tooze, A. (2018). *Crashed: How a Decade of Financial Crises Changed the World*. Viking.

- Coates, T-N. (2017). *We Were Eight Years in Power: An American Tragedy*. One World.

- The French Revolution (1789-1799): Various historical accounts.

- The Russian Revolution (1917): Various historical accounts.

- Reports from the World Economic Forum, International Monetary Fund (IMF), and Organisation for Economic Co-operation and Development (OECD) on wealth inequality and economic policy.

- *The Panama Papers* (2016). International Consortium of Investigative Journalists. [Online] Available at: https://www.icij.org/investigations/panama-papers/

- *The Pandora Papers* (2021). International Consortium of Investigative Journalists. [Online] Available at: https://www.icij.org/investigations/pandora-papers/

- *The Arab Spring* (2010-2012): Various political and economic analyses.

- Brexit's Economic Impact: Reports from the UK Parliament and European Commission.

- Trump's Supreme Court Appointments: U.S. Senate records and judicial impact studies.

- The Great Irish Famine (1845-1852): Historical analyses and Irish government archives.

- The Troubles in Northern Ireland (1960s-1998): Peace agreements, political analyses, and historical records.

- Case studies on modern populist movements, including Trumpism, Brexit, Le Pen's National Rally, and the Dutch Party for Freedom.

- Reports on corporate influence in politics from Transparency International and The Centre for Responsive Politics.

These references provide further reading for those interested in exploring the topics of economic inequality, historical revolutions, and the consequences of wealth concentration in greater depth.

www.ingramcontent.com/pod-product-compliance
Lightning Source LLC
Chambersburg PA
CBHW051216120626
46547CB00013B/1371